CARIBBEAN PALEO

CARIBBEAN PALEO

75 Wholesome Dishes Celebrating Tropical Cuisine and Culture

ALTHEA BROWN

Founder of metemgee.com

First published in 2023 by
Page Street Publishing Co.
27 Congress Street, Suite 1511
Salem, MA 01970
www.pagestreetpublishing.com

Distributed by Macmillan, sales in Canada by The Canadian Manda Group.

27 26 25 24 23 1 2 3 4 5

ISBN-13: 978-1-64567-890-8
ISBN-10: 1-64567-890-3

Library of Congress Control Number: 2022917771

Cover and book design by Laura Benton for Page Street Publishing Co.
Photography by Althea Brown

Printed and bound in USA

Page Street Publishing protects our planet by donating to nonprofits like The Trustees, which focuses on local land conservation.

DEDICATION

FOR MY LATE GRANNY INEZ AND
MY LATE GRANDMOTHER EVELYN

AND ALL THE WOMEN WHO MADE MAGIC IN THE KITCHEN
BECAUSE OF WHAT YOU TAUGHT THEM.

CONTENTS

FOREWORD

I love food. My relentless preoccupation with planning, researching and cooking my next meal borders on obsession. But it took me a long time to admit that I can't just eat whatever looks delicious. Over decades of experience, I learned that certain foods make me feel ill—and I can't continue pretending that I'm just a serial victim of food poisoning every time I eat pasta or bread.

In 2010, I started exploring the Paleo diet, a new-to-me way of eating that prioritizes nutritious, unprocessed ingredients. Despite agonizing over giving up noodles and Chinese dumplings, I was determined to solve the mystery of my food intolerances, so I threw myself into searching for and cooking recipes that fit this approach to food. And surprise, surprise: I felt healthier and more energetic.

At the same time, I realized that if I wanted to enjoy meals that were both Paleo-compatible and tasted authentically like the traditional immigrant comfort foods I craved, I'd have to make them myself. And that's how I decided to create my recipe blog, Nom Nom Paleo, back in 2010. Since then, I've created an award-winning cooking app, written bestselling cookbooks, launched a line of food products, and steadily cranked out recipes for our readers.

To stay inspired in the kitchen, I turn to similarly food-obsessed recipe developers in the Paleo community. So when Althea Brown's smiling face and drool-worthy food popped up on the Official Whole30® Recipes' Instagram feed a few years ago, I became an instant superfan. Like me, Althea adopted a Paleo lifestyle begrudgingly; both of us had realized that some of our favorite childhood foods caused us to feel sick—and we weren't going to give up on the full-flavored and fiery foods that we loved. (After all, life is too short to choke down bland food.) And just as I want to pass my love for Asian foods and culture to my kids, Althea prioritizes cooking Guyanese cuisine at home so her three adorable children will know and love the dishes she grew up eating.

But our differences in cooking style, culinary heritage and flavor profiles also made me stop and take notice of Althea's incredible dishes. Through Althea's website, I've been introduced to amazing Caribbean recipes that I likely wouldn't have encountered otherwise. From spicy Guyanese garlic pork to fragrant bhunjal chicken, each dish I've made has been a stunner. I eagerly anticipate my virtual peeks inside Althea's kitchen; every time I visit, I can feel her passion for making sure these traditional dishes remain true to what she savored in her childhood. Althea inspires me to be a better cook—and she encourages me to season more abundantly with spices and aromatics, too.

Over the years, I've learned so much about Caribbean cooking from Althea—and still do. Every morning when I check her TikTok or Instagram, I see Althea cooking up something delicious that makes my mouth water. I love that she takes the time to explain her process, as well as the ingredients and origins of the dishes she's making—including introducing me to the astounding versatility of plantains. And yes, I totally support her choice to wash her chicken before she cooks it!

When I'm scrolling through her blog or social channels, I often find myself wishing I was Althea's next-door neighbor. There's nothing I'd love more than to wander over to Althea's house, take in the sights, sounds and smells of her kitchen, and watch her cook something delicious that we can munch on while we chat about work, kids and food.

Luckily, I can now do the next best thing: cook from Althea's amazing debut cookbook! *Caribbean Paleo* is a treasure trove of indispensable basics like Green Seasoning (page 131), Jerk Sauce (page 140) and Curry Paste (page 143) as well as lip-smacking crowd pleasers like Plantain Beef Patties (page 62), Hot and Sticky Tamarind Wings (page 26) and Sugar Roti (page 123). Trust me, they're all winners.

I am so excited for all of you to try Althea's recipes. Make these dishes for your family, and without even leaving your own home, you can take a virtual trip to the Caribbean—or better yet, Althea's kitchen!

–MICHELLE TAM,
New York Times bestselling author and founder
of Nom Nom Paleo

INTRODUCTION

I was born and raised in Georgetown, Guyana. My family immigrated when I was 18 years old. The fact that I've now lived longer in the U.S. than I have in my birth country is still daunting to me. I grew up as a Caribbean person. I was taught in school that Guyana was as much a part of the Caribbean as any other island in the Caribbean Sea. Yet somehow, when I moved to America, I became South American. "Where are you from?" is a question I am asked too often to count. At first, I answered proudly that I was from the Caribbean, but people followed up with, "Which island?" Then I started saying I'm from Guyana. Which sounded so much like Ghana that the next reply was almost always, "Ahh, you are African." I now tell people I am from South America.

I am telling you this because it is important to place my recipes within the context of Caribbean food. I am a Caribbean woman, cooking Caribbean food, who just happened to be born in South America. If this boggles your mind, you can thank the British, who strategically isolated Guyana from its South American neighbors and connected it to the other British colonies in the Caribbean. So, although geographically we are South Americans, we live and breathe Caribbean culture.

My recipes are influenced tremendously by the diversity in Guyana and the Caribbean region. There are six races (ethnic groups) in Guyana: Amerindians (our indigenous people), Afro-Guyanese, Indo-Guyanese, Chinese, Portuguese and Europeans. This ethnographic make-up is similar to many other Caribbean countries that have a history of British colonization.

Caribbean food, like many cultural foods, has its similarities, but recipes can vary by country. Although the recipes in this book are mainly Guyanese, some are also influenced by other Caribbean countries. For example, Jerk Chicken Under a Brick (page 16) is directly influenced by Jamaican jerk. Macaroni Pie (page 15) is what Trinidadians call mac and cheese. And every Caribbean country has their version of stew and curry. While these dishes are similar, ingredients may vary depending on the country of influence. When we make spicy food in Guyana, we use wiri wiri peppers, small cherry shaped hot peppers. Scotch bonnet peppers are used in Jamaican cooking, and in Trinidad it is pimento. Therefore, while Caribbean dishes are sometimes lumped together, they are often not exactly the same and sometimes even have different names.

Now that you know I am Guyanese and Caribbean, you must be wondering, "What's Caribbean Paleo?"

In 2015, I was diagnosed with acid reflux and put on a proton pump inhibitor regimen. To say that I had no idea that the way I ate was making me sick is an understatement. I grew up eating roti for breakfast every day. Surely, I thought, roti couldn't be causing my acid reflux. In fact, when a coworker first started talking to me about the Paleo diet, I rolled my eyes in my mind and brushed her off.

Fast-forward to a few months later when the acid reflux wasn't getting better and the medication became do-or-die—I either took it or felt like I was going to die—I started to listen.

To get things started, my coworker recommended I follow an elimination protocol to see which foods might not work well for me. I wasn't familiar with elimination protocols and spent the rest of the afternoon at my desk googling exactly that. This is when I found tons of information about the Whole30. I decided I would start the Whole30 that weekend. The rules were available for free online, so I jumped right in and never looked back. Doing the Whole30 helped me identify that gluten, processed sugars and some grains make me sick. The Whole30 changed my life so much that in 2020 I became a Whole30 Certified Coach and in 2022 I was named Whole30 Coach Innovator of the Year because of all the work I've done to bring Whole30-compatible Caribbean dishes to my community and the Whole30 community.

While I love all the things Whole30 and Paleo have taught me about the food I eat and its impact on my gut health, it took almost 4 years after that initial Whole30 in 2015, and many subsequent Whole30s for me to start saying that I am Paleo. And even still, I say I am Paleo-ish, because I still eat some grains and processed foods occasionally. I wish there was a well-known way to describe a diet (meaning how I eat and not how I eat to lose weight) that prioritizes whole foods that work for your body, without labeling it one thing or another. Until then, I will remain Paleo-ish.

Let's talk a little about Caribbean food and Paleo. While this book is called *Caribbean Paleo,* and some of the recipes have been adapted to fit the Paleo protocol, most recipes needed no adjustments because Caribbean recipes are mostly made from whole foods and fresh ingredients. This book is a celebration of our food, with a few tweaks to honor the way I eat. I hope you find it as useful as I do.

Althea Brown

MY CARIBBEAN FAVES

This first chapter is a compilation of all my favorite Caribbean Paleo dishes. All these dishes have been transformed from a traditional recipe to be Paleo. They cover a variety of categories, from main proteins like Chinese-Inspired Roast Chicken (page 24) to stand-alone dishes like Pumpkin Rice (page 19). These dishes are some of the first things I remixed when I started my Paleo journey, and I am excited for you to try them.

If you make nothing else in this book, please try the recipes in this chapter, specifically Jerk Chicken Under a Brick (page 16), Macaroni Pie (page 15) and Shrimp Chow Mein (page 25). These are my favorite recipes and the ones I'm most proud of—especially Macaroni Pie. I had an idea that I could make a grain- and dairy-free macaroni dish. I wrote out the recipe how I imagined it would work. To my surprise, when I tested the recipe, it needed no tweaks. It is creamy and well seasoned with a tiny bit of heat, and it is just delicious. I hope you give it a try!

MACARONI PIE

Macaroni pie is what some Caribbean countries call mac and cheese. The difference between a Caribbean macaroni pie and an American mac and cheese is that macaroni pie is well seasoned, sometimes contains vegetables like bell peppers, and the best pies are a little spicy. I've had macaroni pie with scallions, bell peppers, corn, lots of fresh herbs and a kick of heat. This is my Paleo macaroni pie made with cassava flour pasta, a creamy cassava-based sauce, almond ricotta, seasoning and a tiny bit of heat. It is creamy and so comforting.

Makes: 6 servings
Cook Time: 45 minutes

8 oz (226 g) cassava elbow noodles
¼ cup (55 g) coconut oil
2 tbsp (30 g) cassava flour
1 cup (240 ml) full-fat coconut milk
1 cup (240 ml) almond or cashew milk
1 tsp spicy brown mustard
1 tbsp (7 g) onion powder
1 tsp garlic powder
1 tsp salt
¼ tsp black pepper
¼ tsp smoked paprika
1 cup (250 g) almond ricotta or similar nut cheese
3 eggs, beaten
¼ cup (15 g) Italian parsley, finely chopped
2 wiri wiri peppers, finely chopped (optional)

To make the macaroni pie, preheat the oven to 350°F (175°C) and grease a baking dish. Cook the noodles according to the instructions on the package, then add them to a large mixing bowl and set aside. In a saucepan over medium-low heat, heat the coconut oil. Add the cassava flour and cook over medium heat for about 2 minutes, then whisk in the coconut milk and almond milk. Continue cooking, whisking constantly, until the mixture thickens, about 3 minutes.

Remove the sauce from the heat, then whisk in the spicy brown mustard, onion powder, garlic powder, salt, black pepper and smoked paprika. Then add the almond ricotta and continue to whisk until smooth with small chunks of the ricotta cheese. Reserve half a cup (120 ml) of the sauce and set aside. To the large bowl containing the cooked pasta that you set aside earlier, add the remaining sauce. Add the beaten eggs, chopped parsley and wiri wiri peppers (if using), and mix together well. Pour the mixture into the prepared baking dish, top with the reserved ½ cup (120 ml) of cheese sauce and bake for 45 minutes, or until the top is slightly browned and no longer wet. Remove from the oven and let cool for 10 minutes before serving.

NOTES: If you want to increase the amount of veggies in this dish, you may add ½ cup (75 g) of diced bell peppers, ½ cup (65 g) of diced carrots and ½ cup (75 g) of green peas (if peas are part of your Paleo diet).

This recipe has been doubled in the accompanying image.

JERK CHICKEN UNDER A BRICK

When most people think about Caribbean food, they think about jerk chicken. Jerk is not just a seasoning or flavor but also a method of cooking that originated in Jamaica, much like barbecue is a method of cooking as well as a flavor. To make authentic jerk chicken, you must season the meat with pimento berries (allspice) as well as grill the chicken over pimento wood. I was introduced to jerk chicken at a birthday party while I was in high school. Prior to this, I had never even heard about jerk anything. The next time I ate jerk chicken was after moving to New York City with my family many years later. Every Friday night my uncle Moses brought home jerk chicken from a little spot at the junction of Flatbush and Nostrand Avenues in Brooklyn. The flavors of that chicken were bold and spicy. We ate it while huffing air into our mouths to cool down the heat and licking our fingers because it was so tasty. I hope you enjoy this recipe the same as we did back then.

Makes: 6–8 servings
Cook Time: 1 hour

1 whole young chicken (about 5 lb [2.25 kg]), backbone removed

2 tbsp (30 ml) avocado oil or similar oil, divided

1 tsp kosher salt, divided

1 cup (240 ml) Jerk Seasoning (page 132), divided

¼ cup (60 ml) lime juice (about 2 limes), divided

2 heavy bricks wrapped in aluminum foil or a heavy cast iron skillet

To Serve

Jerk Sauce (page 140)

Sautéed Callaloo (page 90)

Seasoned Cauliflower Rice (page 89)

Pan-Fried Sweet Plantains (page 139)

Prepare a large bowl or pan for marinating the chicken.

On a clean surface, turn the chicken breast side down and pat dry, then add 1 tablespoon (15 ml) of the avocado oil, ½ teaspoon of the kosher salt, half of the Jerk Seasoning and half of the lime juice. Rub to coat the entire inside of the chicken.

Flip the chicken over, so that it is breast side up. Pat dry, then add the remaining oil, lime juice, Jerk Seasoning and salt. Cover as much of the chicken skin as possible. Then rub the marinade into the neck cavity and under any loose skin. Cover and marinate in the refrigerator overnight.

An hour before you are ready to cook, remove the chicken from the refrigerator and allow it to come up to room temperature. Preheat your grill to 450°F (230°C).

Place the chicken skin side down on the grill, then place the two bricks on top of the chicken. Cover the grill and cook for 30 minutes, then remove the bricks and flip the chicken using tongs. Return the bricks to the chicken and continue to cook covered for another 30 minutes, or until a thermometer inserted into the thighs reads 165°F (75°C). For fall-off-the-bone doneness, let the internal temp of the chicken thighs reach 180°F (82°C) by cooking it for 45 minutes on each side instead.

Remove the bricks from the chicken, then remove the chicken from the grill and let it rest for 10 minutes before carving it up and serving with some Jerk Sauce (page 140), Sautéed Callaloo (page 90), Seasoned Cauliflower Rice (page 89) and Pan-Fried Sweet Plantains (page 139).

NOTE: I bought the bricks for this recipe from a home improvement store. If you don't have access to heavy bricks or a cast iron skillet to use for this recipe, you can simply follow all the grilling instructions but skip placing the bricks on top of the chicken.

PUMPKIN RICE

Rice dishes are a staple in the Caribbean. Not having rice while on a Paleo diet was initially quite a challenge for me, until I started playing with riced vegetables. This recipe is my grain-free take on Guyanese pumpkin rice, with dried shrimp. I was amazed at how close it is to the original rice dish, and it became an instant favorite in my home. The pumpkin I am using in this recipe is calabaza squash, also called Caribbean pumpkin. It can be substituted with butternut or kabocha squash.

Makes: 4 servings
Cook Time: 20 minutes

2 tbsp (28 g) coconut oil
½ yellow onion, diced
1½ tsp (10 g) kosher salt, plus a pinch
2 medium tomatoes, diced
3 cloves (12 g) garlic, grated
2 cups (270 g) diced calabaza squash, butternut squash or kabocha squash
¼ tsp black pepper
1 sprig thyme or 1 tbsp (3 g) dried thyme
20 oz (547 g) frozen riced cauliflower
1 cup (240 ml) canned coconut milk
1 cup (240 ml) water
¼ cup (20 g) dried shrimp (optional)
5–6 Thai basil leaves or Italian basil leaves, finely chopped

To Serve

Pan-Fried Sweet Plantains (page 139)

In a skillet over medium heat, heat the coconut oil. Add the onion and a pinch of kosher salt. Cook until the onion becomes translucent, about 1 minute. Add the tomatoes, garlic and remaining salt. Continue to cook uncovered until the tomatoes are mushy, about 5 minutes.

Next, add the squash, black pepper and thyme. Mix well. Cook uncovered, stirring occasionally, until any liquid cooks down and the squash softens, about 5 minutes. Then add in the riced cauliflower and mix. Increase the heat to high. Cook for a few minutes to toast the cauliflower rice, stirring once or twice. Add the coconut milk, water, dried shrimp (if using) and basil and mix until combined. Bring to a boil, then reduce the heat to medium, cover and continue to cook, stirring often, until most of the liquid cooks down, about 10 minutes. Remove from the heat and serve hot with a side of Pan-Fried Sweet Plantains (page 139).

SPICY FISH CURRY WITH GREEN MANGOES

Caribbean-style fish curry is madras-based (also known as spicy yellow curry) and loaded with flavor. I love making this spicy, dark and rich curry, and just digging into it with my fingers. The addition of the green mangoes gives it a tartness similar to lemon and is absolutely delicious. This is my mother's original recipe and is naturally Paleo, but please check the ingredients lists if using store-bought curries and spice blends, to ensure there are no additives or sneaky ingredients that are not Paleo-friendly.

Makes: 4 servings
Cook Time: 20 minutes

24 oz (680 g) salmon steaks
1 tsp kosher salt
¼ cup (60 ml) Spicy Green Seasoning (page 131)
1 cup (240 ml) avocado oil or other high-heat oil suitable for frying
1 cup (240 g) cassava flour
1 tsp onion powder
1 tsp garlic powder
1 small yellow onion, cut into halves
3 scallions
5 cloves (20 g) garlic
½ cup (8 g) cilantro
2 wiri wiri peppers or ½ Scotch bonnet pepper
3 tbsp (18 g) Curry Powder (page 152)
1 tbsp (5 g) ground coriander
1 tsp paprika
1 tsp Geera (page 157)
½ tsp Garam Masala (page 151)
2½ cups (600 ml) water, divided
4 baby green mangoes, skins on and pits removed
2 bay leaves

To Serve
¼ cup (4 g) cilantro
Toasted Cauliflower Rice (page 136)

Prep the salmon steaks by removing any scales and washing them. Then pat dry, sprinkle with kosher salt and rub with Spicy Green Seasoning. Cover and let marinate for at least 30 minutes or overnight in the refrigerator. Remove from the refrigerator 1 hour before cooking and let the marinated fish come up to room temperature.

In a frying pan or skillet over high heat, heat the avocado oil. On a plate, combine the cassava flour, onion powder and garlic powder. Pat the marinated salmon steaks dry to remove any moisture and excess Spicy Green Seasoning to prevent burning. Then dredge the salmon steaks in the cassava flour mixture, dusting off any excess. Add the lightly floured salmon to the hot oil and cook for 1 to 2 minutes, or until the salmon is golden brown. Remove from the oil and drain on a few paper towels. Reserve 2 tablespoons (30 ml) of the oil used to fry the fish.

To a food processor, add the onion, scallions, garlic, cilantro and wiri wiri peppers and blend until smooth. Then transfer to a bowl. Add the Curry Powder, ground coriander, paprika, Geera, Garam Masala and ½ cup (120 ml) of water. Mix to form a paste-like texture, called a masala.

Warm a clean skillet over medium-high heat. Add the 2 reserved tablespoons (30 ml) of the oil used to fry the fish to the pan. When the oil is hot, but not smoking, add the masala to the oil. Cook, stirring often so that it does not burn. Cook for 5 minutes, or until the masala is dry and thick and most of the liquid has cooked off. Then add the green mangoes and bay leaves. Continue to cook while stirring for another minute.

Add 2 cups (480 ml) of water. Stir to remove any stuck-on masala from the bottom of the pan. Increase the heat to high and bring the curry up to a boil. Once the sauce starts to boil, submerge the fried fish steaks into the curry, making sure that the curry sauce covers the fish steaks. Reduce the heat to low, cover and let simmer for 20 minutes, or until the mangoes are soft and a bit mushy. Garnish with the cilantro and serve with Toasted Cauliflower Rice (page 136).

NOTE: To adjust the heat, use 1 wiri wiri pepper or ¼ habanero, or omit them altogether.

OVEN-BRAISED OXTAIL

Oxtail is one of the Caribbean's favorite cuts of meat, and it is one you will want to take your time with. In this recipe, the oxtail is cooked low and slow until the meat is fall-off-the-bone tender. Traditionally, braised oxtail or oxtail stew is made by browning the meat in a brown sugar caramel (also called browning). In this Paleo recipe, I replaced the sugar caramel with coconut aminos. Coconut aminos add color and a hint of sweetness to balance out the flavors.

Makes: 4 servings
Cook Time: 4 hours

1 tsp sea salt
1 tsp garlic powder
1 tsp smoked paprika
1 tsp onion powder
¼ cup (60 ml) Basic Green Seasoning (page 131)
3 lb (1.4 kg) oxtail, trimmed of excess fat and sliced into 2-inch (5-cm)-thick pieces
1 tbsp (15 ml) avocado oil
¼ cup (60 ml) coconut aminos
1 large onion, sliced
4 cloves (16 g) garlic, sliced
1 tsp tomato paste
6 cups (1.4 L) water or beef bone broth
2 cups (128 g) portabella mushrooms, sliced
1 large carrot, peeled and sliced

To Serve

Seasoned Cauliflower Rice (page 89)
Pan-Fried Sweet Plantains (page 139)

In a large bowl, combine the sea salt, garlic powder, smoked paprika, onion powder and Basic Green Seasoning. Add the oxtail and mix until the oxtail is fully covered in the seasoning. Cover and let marinate for 30 minutes or overnight in the refrigerator for best results.

Preheat the oven to 350°F (175°C). In a Dutch oven over medium-high heat, heat the avocado oil. Add the coconut aminos and cook for 30 seconds, or until the aminos become frothy. Then add the seasoned oxtail to the frothy coconut aminos. Cook, turning often, until browned on all sides. Work in batches if necessary.

Add the onion, garlic and tomato paste and continue to cook, stirring often, about 2 minutes, or until the onion is translucent and a little brown. Stir in the water, ensuring the oxtails are completely submerged. Cover and bring up to a boil, then transfer to the preheated oven.

Cook for 3 hours, then add the mushrooms and carrot. Cover and continue to cook for another hour, or until the oxtail is fall-off-the-bone tender. Scoop the fat from the surface of the sauce with a spoon and discard.

Serve over Seasoned Cauliflower Rice (page 89) and with a side of Pan-Fried Sweet Plantains (page 139).

CHINESE-INSPIRED ROAST CHICKEN

Caribbean people will fight you about how tasty Caribbean Chinese food is. They will tell you that some of the best Chinese food is made in the Caribbean. And they won't be lying. Guyanese Chinese fried rice has a hint of sweetness that I thought only demerara brown sugar could deliver. The addition of this sugar into sauces and marinades is what gives Guyanese Chinese food its signature taste. Surprisingly, coconut aminos does the same thing. So, I use it in all my Chinese-inspired dishes to make them Paleo. In this soy and refined-sugar-free version of Caribbean Chinese roast chicken, I've created a flavor profile that is identical to the traditional recipe and is gentle on the gut by swapping out soy sauce and cane sugar for coconut aminos.

Makes: 4 servings
Cook Time: 65 minutes

Roast Chicken

4 chicken leg quarters
½ cup (120 ml) coconut aminos
1 cup (240 ml) water
½ cup (120 ml) red wine vinegar or coconut vinegar
½ cup (120 ml) orange juice (about 2 navel oranges)
2-inch (5-cm) piece ginger root, grated
8 cloves (32 g) garlic, grated
1 tbsp (10 g) Chinese five spice
1 tsp kosher salt
1 tsp shiitake mushroom powder
2 tbsp (30 ml) avocado oil
2 scallions, thinly sliced

Sauce

¼ cup (60 ml) coconut aminos
½ tsp Chinese five spice
¼ tsp ground ginger
2 tbsp (30 ml) Paleo-friendly ketchup

To Serve

Seasoned Cauliflower Rice (page 89)
Pickled Cucumbers (page 144)

To make the roast chicken, place the chicken leg quarters in a large bowl.

In a small mixing bowl, combine the coconut aminos, water, red wine vinegar, orange juice, grated ginger root, garlic, Chinese five spice, kosher salt, shiitake mushroom powder and avocado oil. Mix to make a brine. Pour the brine over the top of the chicken leg quarters, making sure the chicken is fully submerged. Brine in the refrigerator for 24 hours.

Remove the chicken from the refrigerator and the brine 1 hour before cooking and allow it to come up to room temperature.

Preheat the oven to 450°F (230°C). Place an oven-safe rack on a baking sheet.

Remove any excess seasoning from the chicken leg quarters and pat them dry. Then place the chicken skin side up on the rack set on the baking sheet. Roast for 30 minutes, then flip over and continue to roast for another 25 minutes, or until the chicken has an internal temperature of 165°F (75°C).

To make the sauce, combine the coconut aminos, Chinese five spice, ground ginger and ketchup in a small mixing bowl and mix well. Brush the chicken with the sauce and continue to cook for 5 minutes. Flip over the chicken and repeat. Remove from the oven, rest for 5 minutes, then garnish with the sliced scallions.

Serve your Chinese-Inspired Roast Chicken with a side of Seasoned Cauliflower Rice (page 89) and Pickled Cucumbers (page 144).

NOTE: Traditionally, Chinese roast chicken is served chopped up on top of fried rice with cucumbers and shredded cabbage. If you have a butcher knife sharp enough to chop through the bones and you really want to have that look, feel free to give it a try. I live for this kind of nostalgia. If not, you can cut your leg quarters into thighs and drumsticks and serve it like that.

SHRIMP CHOW MEIN

If anyone asked me what my favorite dish was when I was growing up, I proudly said chicken chow mein. Guyanese-style chicken chow mein is one of those dishes that I dove headfirst into every time my mom made it. Fast-forward to now and my gluten-free, Paleo-ish life: when the craving for chow mein hits, I make this simple but delicious stir-fry. It is completely gluten-free and Paleo. I use yellow squash noodles because they look similar to chow mein noodles. I know the way I cook this dish is more akin to lo mein and not traditional Chinese chow mein, but in Guyana and in the Caribbean we call this dish chow mein. So here it is: my Guyanese-style Paleo Shrimp Chow Mein.

Makes: 4 servings
Cook Time: 10 minutes

1 lb (454 g) large shrimp, peeled and deveined, tails removed
½ tsp kosher salt
6 cloves (24 g) garlic, grated
1-inch (2.5-cm) piece ginger, grated
1 wiri wiri or habanero pepper, minced (optional)
1 tsp Chinese five spice
2 tbsp (30 ml) avocado oil or similar, divided
1 tbsp (15 ml) toasted sesame oil
½ small onion, diced
4 scallions, thinly sliced, white and green parts separated
½ red bell pepper, julienned
5 Chinese long beans, cut into 2-inch (5-cm) pieces and blanched
1 large carrot, julienned
2 bok choy, chopped
¼ cup (60 ml) coconut aminos
4 yellow squash, spiralized

To Serve

Pickled Cucumbers (page 144)

In a mixing bowl, combine the shrimp, kosher salt, garlic, ginger, wiri wiri pepper (if using) and Chinese five spice. Mix and let marinate for 15 minutes.

To a hot skillet or wok over high heat, add 1 tablespoon (15 ml) of avocado and toasted sesame oils. Then add the marinated shrimp and cook for 2 minutes on each side, or until opaque and pink. Remove from the wok and set aside.

Next, return the skillet or wok to high heat and add 1 tablespoon (15 ml) of avocado oil to the wok, followed by the diced onion and the white parts of the scallions. Cook for about 2 minutes, or until the onion becomes a little brown and soft, then add the red bell pepper and cook for 1 minute, stirring often. Next add the Chinese long beans and the carrot and continue to cook for about 1 minute. Then add the bok choy. Cook for another minute before adding back in the shrimp, followed by the coconut aminos. Continue to cook until any liquids cook off, about 2 minutes. Then add the yellow squash noodles and green parts of the scallions. Mix and immediately remove from the heat. Serve with a few slices of Pickled Cucumbers (page 144).

NOTE: I use a very simple vegetable spiralizer called the Veggetti to turn my yellow squash into noodles. I highly recommend it, as it is cheap and easy to use. However, if you don't have access to a spiralizer, you can thinly julienne your squash noodles.

HOT AND STICKY TAMARIND WINGS

Tamarind is such a key flavor in Caribbean cuisine that tamarind wings just make sense to me. The tangy tamarind, with the spicy wiri wiri along with the little bit of sweetness from the coconut aminos, creates a flavor that makes you want to eat this batch of wings in one sitting. For even more of a flavah punch, try it with some Wiri Wiri Ranch Dressing (page 155). These cook up quickly in the air fryer, no deep-frying required. I just love that going Paleo helped me to simplify how I prepare so many of my recipes.

Makes: 4 servings (30 wings)
Cook Time: 45 minutes

Chicken Wings

2 lb (908 g) chicken wings, drums and flats separated

¼ cup (60 ml) lemon juice (about 1 lemon)

2 tbsp (30 ml) avocado oil

¾ tsp kosher salt

1 tsp garlic powder

1 tbsp (7 g) onion powder

½ tsp smoked paprika

3 scallions, thinly sliced

Tamarind Glaze

2 tbsp (60 g) seedless tamarind paste

1¼ cups (300 ml) water, divided

¼ cup (60 ml) coconut aminos

2 wiri wiri peppers or ½ habanero pepper, finely chopped

1 tsp tapioca flour

Salt to taste

In a large bowl, coat the chicken wings with lemon juice and avocado oil. Then add the kosher salt, garlic powder, onion powder and smoked paprika and mix together until all sides of the chicken wings are covered with seasoning. Cover and let marinate in the refrigerator for at least 1 hour or overnight for best results.

Remove the chicken from the refrigerator 30 minutes before cooking and let it come up to room temperature.

Preheat the air fryer to 400°F (205°C).

Add the chicken wings to a greased air fryer basket or tray and air fry for 15 minutes, then flip and air fry for another 15 minutes.

To make the tamarind glaze, combine the seedless tamarind paste, 1 cup (240 ml) of water, coconut aminos and wiri wiri peppers in a small saucepan. Over medium heat, cook the mixture, stirring, until the tamarind paste loosens and dissolves into the liquids. Continue to cook for 5 minutes, or until bubbly.

Make a slurry by combining ¼ cup (60 ml) of water and the tapioca flour. Add the slurry to the bubbling tamarind sauce while stirring vigorously to avoid lumps. Remove from the heat, then add salt to taste.

After air frying the wings, coat the wings in the tamarind glaze, then return the wings to the air fryer for an additional 5 minutes on each side. Then remove the wings from the air fryer, toss in any remaining glaze, garnish with sliced scallion and serve hot.

SAUCY BAKED CHICKEN

I grew up eating baked chicken on special occasions, like birthdays and holidays. It was not an everyday meal. My mom marinated chicken leg quarters in the refrigerator for a few days and then baked them. My mom's baked chicken had a dark, rich color from the addition of cassareep (a soy sauce–like cooking ingredient made from cassava extract). It has a little bit of sweetness because she always added a pinch of brown sugar when seasoning most meats. And most importantly it was fall-off-the-bone tender. This is my version of her recipe. I use coconut aminos in my marinade to replace the cassareep and brown sugar, therefore making the recipe completely Paleo but still true to the flavors of my mom's dish.

Makes: 4 servings
Cook Time: 1 hour 35 minutes

1 yellow onion, peeled and cut into chunks
6 cloves (24 g) garlic, peeled
¼ cup (15 g) Italian parsley
1-inch (2.5-cm) piece ginger, peeled
3 wiri wiri peppers, veins and seeds removed
¼ tsp ground cinnamon
¼ tsp nutmeg
5 sprigs thyme, leaves removed from stems
1 tbsp (15 ml) red wine vinegar
¼ cup (60 ml) coconut aminos
1 tsp kosher salt
3 lb (1.4 kg) chicken leg quarters

To Serve

Caribbean Yellow Rice (page 93)
Deviled Eggs Plantain Salad (page 77)

In a food processor, combine the yellow onion, garlic, parsley, ginger, wiri wiri peppers, cinnamon, nutmeg and thyme. Then drizzle in the red wine vinegar and coconut aminos. Blend until smooth, about 1 minute.

Sprinkle the kosher salt over the chicken and place in a bowl. Add the marinade and mix until every piece of chicken is coated with the marinade, getting some under the chicken skin if possible. Cover and let marinate for 30 minutes or overnight in the refrigerator, for best results. Remove the chicken from the refrigerator 1 hour before cooking and let it come up to room temperature.

Preheat the oven to 375°F (190°C).

Place the chicken skin side up in a single layer in a baking dish. Drizzle any remaining marinade over the chicken. Cover with aluminum foil and bake for 1 hour. After 1 hour, uncover, increase the heat to 450°F (230°C) and continue to bake for another 15 minutes. Flip the chicken thighs over, baste with pan juices and continue to cook uncovered for another 15 minutes. Then flip the chicken over again and baste again with pan juices. Continue to cook for another 5 minutes, or until the pan juices cook down and a thick sauce remains.

Let rest for 10 minutes before serving. Serve with Caribbean Yellow Rice (page 93) and Deviled Eggs Plantain Salad (page 77).

ROASTED JERK SALMON

Looking for a quick main dish that is sure to impress anyone? Then try this Roasted Jerk Salmon recipe. All you need is some homemade Paleo Jerk Seasoning (page 132) slathered over a nice piece of salmon. Roast it up in the oven and we are in business. This salmon roasts quickly in the oven or air fryer.

Makes: 4 servings
Cook Time: 15 minutes

2 lb (907 g) salmon fillet (skinless or skin-on)
¼ cup (60 ml) lemon juice (about 1 lemon)
2 tbsp (30 ml) avocado oil or similar
3 tbsp (45 ml) Jerk Seasoning (page 132)
½ tsp coarse salt
1 navel orange, sliced, divided
Handful of fresh parsley

To Serve

Cassava Couscous Salad (page 78)

Prepare a greased baking sheet.

Rinse and pat the salmon dry. Then place the salmon fillet skin side down (if using skin-on salmon) on the greased baking sheet. Drizzle generously with lemon juice and avocado oil. Then slather with the Jerk Seasoning and coarse salt. Cover and let marinate for 30 minutes.

Preheat the oven to 400°F (205°C). Add half of the orange slices to the top of the salmon, reserving the rest for garnish. Bake the salmon on the center rack in the oven for 15 minutes. Remove from the oven and let rest for 5 minutes before garnishing with the remaining orange slices and parsley. The salmon will continue to cook as it rests.

Serve the Roasted Jerk Salmon with a side of Cassava Couscous Salad (page 78).

NOTE: To cook the salmon in the air fryer, preheat the air fryer to 400°F (205°C). Add the seasoned fillet to a greased air fryer basket and air fry for 8 minutes. Then remove from the heat and rest for 5 minutes before garnishing and serving.

SOUPS, STEWS AND CURRIES

Soups, stews and curries are everyday Caribbean food. Soups do not have a season. No matter the temperature, we eat soups in the Caribbean. Soup Sunday is also a tradition in many Caribbean countries. My grandmother Inez Glen made the most amazing Beef and Ground Provision Soup (page 35). I share my take on her recipe in this chapter, and I highly recommend that you cozy up with a bowl. It is hearty, nutritious and so filling.

In Guyana, a stew can be as simple as some chicken and vegetables sautéed together, as in the Chicken and Asparagus recipe shared in this chapter (page 50). Or it could be more like a traditional stew made with protein in a sauce, such as my Red Stew Chicken (page 36). Stews are typically served with rice, in this case cauliflower rice or root vegetables, and are an everyday occurrence. You just can't go wrong with a Classic Chicken Stew (page 47).

I grew up eating spicy curries. My mother Sheena is Indo-Guyanese, and her ancestors came to Guyana from India as indentured laborers. Curries and Indian spices were part of my palate from an early age. Back then we ate curry at least once a week. Today, curry dishes are still in regular rotation in my home. Bhunjal Lamb Chops (page 44) is one of my favorite recipes in this chapter. It is a beautiful madras curry with deep notes of garam masala and spices over tender lamb chops. I can't wait for you to try this recipe and the many others shared in this chapter! Let's dig in!

BEEF AND GROUND PROVISION SOUP

Hearty soups are a Caribbean must-have. We do not need cool, cozy weather for soup. In the Caribbean, we eat soups even when it is hot and humid. If you think about it, if we waited for it to be cold to eat soup, we wouldn't get to enjoy all this deliciousness as often as we do. I have so many memories of my late grandmother Inez making this soup on Sundays and serving it up with fufu (crushed plantains). She cooked hers in a traditional pressure cooker, but I make mine in the Instant Pot. Grab your Instant Pot for this recipe that comes together with ease.

Makes: 6 servings
Cook Time: 1 hour 10 minutes

- 2 lb (907 g) beef short ribs
- 1 lb (454 g) beef chuck, cut into large chunks
- 1 tsp garlic powder
- 1 tbsp (7 g) onion powder
- 2 tsp (14 g) kosher salt
- ½ tsp freshly cracked black pepper
- 2 tbsp (30 ml) avocado oil
- 1 large onion, roughly chopped
- 1 head garlic
- 5 large sprigs thyme
- 8–10 cups (2–2.4 L) water
- 1 cassava, peeled and cut into 6 pieces (page 158)
- 1 American sweet potato, peeled and cut into chunks
- 2 yellow plantains, peeled (page 159), each cut into 3 pieces
- 1 Japanese sweet potato, peeled and cut into 6 pieces
- 3–4 eddoes or small taro (optional), peeled and cut into halves
- 2 wiri wiri peppers or similar

Season the beef short ribs and chuck with garlic powder, onion powder, kosher salt and the cracked black pepper and set aside.

Set an 8 quart (7.6 L) or larger Instant Pot to sauté. When the pot is hot, add the avocado oil, then all the seasoned beef and cook for about 5 minutes, stirring often. Then add the onion, garlic, thyme and water. Stir to combine. Then seal up and pressure cook on high for 45 minutes.

Release the pressure using the rapid release function. Then add the cassava and continue to cook using the sauté function. Boil for about 10 minutes, or until the cassava starts to look a little translucent, then add the American sweet potato, yellow plantains, Japanese sweet potato, eddoes (if using) and wiri wiri peppers. Continue to cook until all the ground provisions are fork tender and the cassava is a bit mushy, about 10 minutes. Crush some of the soft cassava and sweet potatoes and mix into the broth to thicken.

NOTES: For this soup, choose a combination of beef with bones and cuts with fat. This will give the soup a rich and delicious broth.

Using whole wiri wiri peppers in this recipe adds flavor without any heat. Avoid crushing the peppers to keep the recipe mild. Crush the peppers and mix them into the soup to make it spicy.

RED STEW CHICKEN

This Red Stew Chicken is a childhood favorite. It is tomato based and has a distinct red color, therefore "red stew." Although in Guyana, this dish is just called chicken stew or stew chicken and we don't use the color to describe it the way they would in Jamaica, for example. I named this recipe Red Stew Chicken simply to distinguish it from Classic Chicken Stew (page 47). My mom made this stew with roti for breakfast. Can you believe it? We ate chicken stew and roti for breakfast and never complained. I mean, we couldn't, because 1. My mother is a Caribbean mother, and 2. It was delicious and filling. Little did I know that this stew is Paleo-friendly, made exactly as my mom does with no tweaks. I can no longer eat my mom's roti, but now I enjoy my own Paleo Potato Roti (page 105), and still eat this for breakfast!

Makes: 4 servings
Cook Time: 45 minutes

2 lb (907 g) skin-on chicken drumsticks and skin-on, bone-in chicken thighs
¼ cup (60 ml) Basic Green Seasoning (page 131)
1 tsp kosher salt, divided
2–3 tbsp (30–45 ml) olive oil
1 large onion, sliced
4 cloves (16 g) garlic, grated
6 tomatoes (500 g), diced
¼ cup (66 g) tomato paste
2 cups (480 ml) water
4 sprigs thyme
2 scallions, thinly sliced

To Serve

Potato Roti (page 105)

Clean and prep the chicken. Remove most of the skin from the drumsticks and all the skin from the thighs. Then pat the chicken dry. Season the chicken with the Basic Green Seasoning and ½ teaspoon of kosher salt. Let it marinate for at least 30 minutes.

Heat a deep skillet over high heat. Add the olive oil and when it is hot, add the sliced onion and cook for about 1 minute, or until the onion starts to brown a little. Then add the garlic, diced tomatoes, tomato paste and ½ teaspoon of salt. Continue to cook, stirring often, until the tomatoes cook down and become mushy, about 3 minutes.

Add the seasoned chicken to the cooked-down tomatoes, in a single layer if possible. Let the chicken cook in the tomatoes, untouched, for about 1 minute. Flip the chicken pieces over and cook untouched for 1 minute. This allows you to fully combine the flavors of the tomato base with the seasoned chicken. Be careful not to burn the chicken or the tomatoes here, as this will change the flavor and color of the final dish.

Cook the chicken with the tomatoes for an additional 10 minutes, while continuing to stir or flip as needed to prevent burning. Then add the water, stirring to remove any stuck-on bits from the bottom of the pan. Add the sprigs of thyme, then spoon some of the sauce over the chicken, cover and continue to cook over high heat for 30 minutes, or until the chicken is cooked all the way through and the sauce thickened. Top with the sliced scallions and serve with Potato Roti (page 105).

CARIBBEAN CHICKEN SOUP

Chicken soup with a pumpkin broth is a match made in heaven. Jamaicans call this cock soup. It is typically made with a soup mix that includes bits of noodles. This soup is perfect for cold fall and winter nights, or rainy days if you are in the tropics. In my Paleo version of this cock soup-inspired Caribbean Chicken Soup, I use chicken and lots of hearty veggies. I use spaghetti squash in place of noodles, and I have to say that it works beautifully. You can double this recipe to make a large pot of soup with plenty of leftovers that you can freeze!

Makes: 4–6 servings
Cook Time: 1 hour

½ whole chicken (about 2½ lb [1.2 kg]), butchered into chunks
1½ tsp (10 g) coarse salt
1 tbsp (15 ml) Basic Green Seasoning (page 131)
1 spaghetti squash
3 tbsp (45 ml) avocado oil, divided
1 yellow onion, diced
5 cloves (20 g) garlic, minced
8 cups (1.9 L) water
2 cups diced calabaza or butternut squash
1 large Japanese sweet potato, peeled and cubed
2 chayote squash, peeled and cubed
2 carrots, peeled and sliced
4 sprigs thyme
¼ tsp turmeric
1 tsp garlic powder
1 tsp onion powder
1 tbsp (11 g) allspice berries
1 whole Scotch bonnet pepper or 2 whole wiri wiri peppers

In a bowl, combine the chicken, ½ teaspoon of coarse salt and Basic Green Seasoning and mix well. Set aside and let marinate for 30 minutes.

Preheat the oven to 450°F (230°C). Line a sheet pan with parchment paper.

Cut the spaghetti squash in half lengthwise and scoop out the guts. Rub the flesh with 1 tablespoon (15 ml) of avocado oil, then add a sprinkle of salt. Place the squash cut side down on the prepared sheet pan and roast for 30 to 45 minutes, or until a fork can easily pierce the skin. Allow to cool, then remove the strands from the skin, place in a bowl and set aside.

While the spaghetti squash is roasting, heat a large stockpot over high heat. When hot, add the remaining 2 tablespoons (30 ml) of oil, the onion and garlic. Cook, stirring once or twice, until the onion starts to brown, about 2 minutes. Then add the chicken. Stir a few times for even cooking and continue to cook until the chicken browns on all sides. Add the water, salt, calabaza squash, Japanese sweet potato, chayote squash, carrots, thyme, turmeric, garlic powder, onion powder and allspice berries. Stir to combine, then cover and bring to a boil. Reduce the heat to medium and continue to cook for about 40 minutes, or until all the veggies are fork tender and the chicken starts to fall off the bones.

Reduce the heat to low, then add the Scotch bonnet pepper. Continue to simmer for another 10 minutes. Remove from the heat.

Add the spaghetti squash strands to individual bowls as you serve to prevent them from getting mushy.

ZUCCHINI STEW

The first time I had zucchini stew was shortly after we moved to the U.S. My mother was busy in the kitchen. When I asked what she was making, she said zucchini stew. She was cooking it the way we cook bottle gourd squash. "After all," she said, "It is a squash!" This is her recipe with one simple adjustment to make it Paleo. I swapped her pinch of brown sugar for some coconut aminos.

Makes: 4 servings
Cook Time: 15 minutes

2 lb (907 g) zucchini
2 tbsp (28 g) coconut oil
1 small yellow onion, diced
4 tomatoes, diced
5 cloves (20 g) garlic, grated
1 tsp salt, divided
1 tbsp (15 ml) coconut aminos
¼ cup (4 g) cilantro, chopped

To Serve
Toasted Cauliflower Rice (page 136)

Peel the zucchinis, scoop out the seeds, then dice the flesh. In a skillet over high heat, heat the coconut oil. Add the onion and cook for about 3 minutes, stirring once or twice. Add the tomatoes, garlic and a pinch of salt. Mix to combine. Cover, reduce the heat to medium, and let cook until the tomatoes are soft and mushy, about 5 minutes.

Toss in the zucchinis. Add the remaining salt and coconut aminos. Give it a good stir, then cover and let steam until the zucchinis are soft but not mushy, no more than 7 minutes. Increase the heat to high and continue to cook for a minute or two to reduce any liquid formed while steaming. Stir in the chopped cilantro. Then remove from the heat and serve over some Toasted Cauliflower Rice (page 136).

PUMPKIN AND SWEET POTATO CURRY

Calabaza squash is commonly called pumpkin in Guyana and the Caribbean. Typically, when I mention pumpkin in recipes, I am referring to calabaza squash. Butternut squash is a great substitute for calabaza squash and used often in Caribbean households in the U.S as pumpkin. My mom makes a delicious pumpkin and potato curry that she serves with hot paratha roti. This is that dish with one swap. I replaced the white potatoes she uses in her version with Caribbean sweet potatoes, and it is absolutely delicious. Golden sweet potatoes also work really well if you do not have access to Caribbean (or Japanese).

Makes: 4 servings
Cook Time: 18 minutes

½ yellow onion, chopped
4 cloves (16 g) garlic
1 tsp Geera (page 157)
1 tsp ground coriander
½ tsp Garam Masala (page 151)
1 tbsp (6 g) Curry Powder (page 152)
3 tbsp (41 g) coconut oil
1 lb (907 g) calabaza squash, peeled and diced
1 Caribbean or Japanese sweet potato, peeled and cut into 1-inch (2.5-cm) cubes
¾ tsp sea salt
¼ cup (60 ml) coconut milk
2 cups (480 ml) water
¼ cup (4 g) cilantro, finely chopped

To Serve
Potato Roti (page 105)

Add the onion and garlic to a food processor and blend until smooth. Then add the Geera, ground coriander, Garam Masala and Curry Powder to the blended onion and garlic. Pulse three to five times, or mix in a separate bowl to prevent the Curry Powder from staining the food processor bowl.

In a large skillet over high heat, heat the coconut oil. Add the curry paste mixture and cook for about 3 minutes, stirring often to prevent burning, until the liquid cooks off. When the curry paste browns and starts to stick to the pan, immediately add the calabaza squash and sweet potatoes, sea salt, coconut milk and water. Mix, using a spoon to free any bits stuck to the bottom of the pan. Cover, then reduce the heat to medium-low and simmer until the sweet potatoes are fork tender, about 15 minutes. Using the back of a spoon, crush half of the calabaza squash pieces, then add the cilantro and mix well. Serve with some Potato Roti (page 105). Rip pieces of the roti to scoop the curry.

BHUNJAL LAMB CHOPS

If you love lamb, then these hot and spicy lamb chops are for you. Bhunjal *is what we (Guyanese) call curry that is cooked down so that the sauce clings to the meat. It is very much like the Indian dish bhuna, and I often wonder if that's where the word comes from, perhaps distorted over the years. This Bhunjal Lamb Chops recipe is heavily influenced by bhunjal chicken, a spicy chicken curry dish popular in Guyana. It is naturally Paleo and delicious. As always, if you are using store-bought spices for this recipe, please read your ingredient labels to ensure that there are no ingredients that are not Paleo-friendly.*

Makes: 4 servings
Cook Time: 20 minutes

8 bone-in lamb chops, about 2 lb (907 g)
¼ cup (60 ml) avocado oil, or similar, divided
2-inch (5-cm) piece ginger, grated
4 cloves (16 g) garlic, grated
1 tbsp (5 g) Geera (page 157)
½ tsp salt
1 tsp paprika
Pinch of cayenne
½ cup (120 g) Curry Paste (page 143)
1 tsp tomato paste
½ cup (120 ml) water

To Serve

Potato Roti (page 105)
Grilled Okra Choka (page 94)

Pat the lamb chops dry, then drizzle with 1 tablespoon (15 ml) of avocado oil. Season the chops with grated ginger, garlic, Geera, salt, paprika and a pinch of cayenne pepper. Let marinate in the refrigerator overnight or for at least 30 minutes.

Rest the chops at room temperature for at least 30 minutes before cooking.

Heat a large skillet over medium-high heat until very hot, then add 3 tablespoons (45 ml) of avocado oil. When the oil is hot but not smoking, add the marinated lamb chops and cook for 3 to 4 minutes before flipping. Cook for another 3 minutes, then remove from the pan and set aside. The chops should have a nice brown sear on both sides.

Add the Curry Paste and tomato paste to the skillet and mix together well. Cook for about 2 minutes to allow the curry paste to come up to temperature, then add the water and continue to cook until bubbly, 1 to 2 minutes. Add back in the lamb chops. Continue to cook for another 2 minutes, then flip the lamb chops over and continue to cook for another 2 minutes. When the sauce cooks down and is thick and clinging to the lamb chops, remove from the heat. Serve with Potato Roti (page 105) and Grilled Okra Choka (page 94).

CLASSIC CHICKEN STEW

Chicken stew is sacred to Guyanese people. It is the base of many combinations of meat and vegetable dishes. A good chicken stew starts with cleaned and prepped chicken that is marinated in Basic Green Seasoning (page 131). When I was growing up, my mom did this step immediately after returning from the market. She then placed her seasoned chicken in the freezer until she was ready to cook it. I love marinating my chicken overnight, but if I'm in a rush, I marinate it while I'm prepping my other ingredients or my side dishes. The major difference between this chicken stew and traditional chicken stew is the use of coconut aminos instead of burnt cane sugar. This makes it Paleo since there is no added refined sugar. Once you've mastered this stew, you can make many variations by adding different vegetables to the chicken base, like I did with my Chicken and Asparagus stew (page 50).

Makes: 4 servings
Cook Time: 30 minutes

2½ lb (1.2 kg) bone-in chicken drumsticks and thighs, skin removed
¼ cup (60 ml) Basic Green Seasoning (page 131)
½ tsp kosher salt
¼ tsp ground ginger
1 tsp garlic powder
1 tsp onion powder
1 tsp smoked paprika
1 tsp tomato paste
1 tsp spicy brown mustard
2 tbsp (30 ml) olive oil
½ cup (120 ml) coconut aminos
4 sprigs thyme
2 medium tomatoes, diced
2 medium potatoes, sliced (optional)
1 carrot, sliced (optional)
1 cup (149 g) mixed bell peppers, sliced (optional)
About 2 cups (480 ml) water

To Serve

Toasted Cauliflower Rice (page 136)
Pan-Fried Sweet Plantains (page 139)

In a bowl, combine the chicken and the Basic Green Seasoning, kosher salt, ground ginger, garlic powder, onion powder, smoked paprika, tomato paste and spicy brown mustard. Mix well and let marinate for at least 30 minutes or overnight in the refrigerator for best results.

Over medium heat, heat a skillet wide enough to cook the chicken in a single layer. When the skillet is hot, heat the olive oil, then add the coconut aminos. The coconut aminos should immediately start to bubble. When the bubbles are vigorous and more than three-quarters of the aminos are frothy, about 2 minutes, add the seasoned chicken to the pan in a single layer. Let the chicken cook untouched for 2 to 3 minutes so that it is browned, then turn each piece and repeat until all the sides of the chicken are brown.

Add the thyme and tomatoes and gently mix. Add the potatoes, carrot and bell peppers (if using) and mix together well. Add the water, cover and increase the heat to high. Bring to a boil and cook for about 5 minutes, then reduce the heat to medium and continue to cook, covered, until the potatoes (if using) are fork tender and the chicken is cooked all the way through. This may take up to 20 minutes.

Taste your stew and add additional salt if needed. Serve over Toasted Cauliflower Rice (page 136) and with a side of Pan-Fried Sweet Plantains (page 139).

NOTE: Coconut aminos vary by brand, and some can be high in sodium. When cooking with coconut aminos, please adjust the salt to taste toward the end of the dish.

PEPPER STEAK

This dish is sure to make its way into your weeknight Paleo lineup. Caribbean food is such a mix of cultures, and Chinese food definitely has a place. Pepper steak is very popular in Jamaican cuisine. Traditional Jamaican pepper steak recipes use browning (a brown sugar caramel) and cornstarch in the sauce. In my version, I use coconut aminos in place of browning and cassava flour in place of cornstarch. These little swaps make the recipe Paleo-friendly but do not compromise the taste of the final dish. It tastes exactly like the original. You really cannot go wrong with steak marinated in Spicy Green Seasoning (page 131), stir-fried with peppers and smothered in coconut aminos!

Makes: 4–6 servings
Cook Time: 20 minutes

1½ lb (681 g) rib-eye steak
¼ cup (60 g) Spicy Green Seasoning (page 131)
½ tsp paprika
¾ tsp kosher salt, divided
2 tbsp (30 ml) avocado oil or similar
1 small onion, sliced
4 cloves (16 g) garlic, thinly sliced
1 red bell pepper, julienned
1 yellow bell pepper, julienned
1 green bell pepper, julienned
½ cup (120 ml) coconut aminos
¼ cup (60 ml) water
1 tsp cassava flour

To Serve

Seasoned Cauliflower Rice (page 89)
Pan-Fried Sweet Plantains (page 139)

Cut the steak against the grain into 3 x ½-inch (8 x 1.3-cm) strips. Then in a bowl, combine the steak, Spicy Green Seasoning, paprika and ½ teaspoon of kosher salt. Mix well and let marinate for 10 minutes.

Heat a large skillet over medium heat and add the avocado oil. When the oil is hot, add the onion and cook until it starts to brown, about 2 minutes. Add the garlic and cook until the garlic gets a little brown, about 1 minute. Add the bell peppers and ¼ teaspoon of salt. Continue to cook for another minute, stirring often, then remove the cooked veggies from the pan and set aside.

Turn the heat up to high. When the pan is hot, add the marinated steak in a single layer and brown on all sides, working in batches if necessary. This should take 3 to 5 minutes total per batch.

Add the coconut aminos to the pan and mix well with the cooked steak. Continue to cook for another 1 to 2 minutes. Make a slurry by mixing the water and cassava flour, ensuring that there are no lumps. Add the slurry to the pan and mix, then add the cooked veggies and mix. Cook for 1 minute, then remove from the heat. The sauce will continue to thicken as it cools.

Serve over Seasoned Cauliflower Rice (page 89) and with a side of Pan-Fried Sweet Plantains (page 139).

CHICKEN AND ASPARAGUS

Growing up in Guyana, most of our weeknight meals were a combination of a vegetable and some protein cooked into what we called a stew. This was then served on a bed of rice. The combinations varied, but the main idea of the dish and this meal were consistent: a stew served over rice. When I moved to the United States, I discovered so many new vegetables that I could add to the rotation. Asparagus and chicken doesn't sound like a Caribbean stew combo, but trust me, it is worth trying. When cooked this way, in all the flavor of the chicken stew, the asparagus is transformed. I love serving this in a bowl over Toasted Cauliflower Rice (page 136), then I cozy up in a chair and dig right in.

Makes: 4 servings
Cook Time: 30 minutes

1½ lb (681 g) boneless, skinless chicken thighs
¼ cup (60 ml) Basic Green Seasoning (page 131)
1 tsp kosher salt
2 tbsp (28 g) coconut oil
¼ cup (60 ml) coconut aminos
1 tsp tomato paste
2 large tomatoes, diced
1 bunch asparagus, cut into 2-inch (5-cm) pieces

To Serve

Toasted Cauliflower Rice (page 136)

Trim any visible fat and cut the chicken thighs roughly into 2 x 2-inch (5 x 5-cm) pieces. In a large bowl, combine the chicken thighs, Basic Green Seasoning and kosher salt. Let marinate for 30 minutes or overnight in the refrigerator if time allows. Remove from the refrigerator an hour before cooking and allow to come to room temperature.

Heat the coconut oil in a skillet on high heat, then add the coconut aminos and tomato paste. Cook until the coconut aminos becomes frothy, about 1 minute. Then add the seasoned chicken and continue to cook over high heat. Let it sit for about 3 minutes without stirring to reduce the liquids, then stir to ensure some of the chicken that was at the top is now on the bottom. Cover and let cook for 5 minutes. At this point, some liquid should form in the pan. Remove the cover and let the liquid cook down, stirring once or twice.

Once all the liquid cooks off, add the tomatoes and asparagus and mix well. Continue to cook over high heat, stirring often until the asparagus is done, about 5 minutes. Then remove from the heat and enjoy in a bowl over Toasted Cauliflower Rice (page 136).

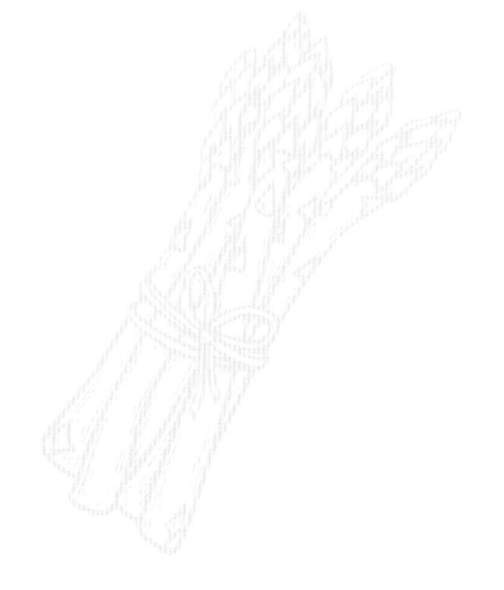

CURRY GOAT

Although curry is popular throughout the Caribbean, curry goat is a signature Jamaican dish. Jamaicans also call this dish mutton curry, although mutton is the name for sheep meat. I started making this Curry Goat when I moved to Colorado and became part of the Caribbean community here, which is made up mostly of Jamaicans. This recipe is exactly how I make it for my Jamaican friends and needed no adjustments to make it Paleo. I love that about some Caribbean dishes. The key to really tasty goat is how you prepare the meat before it is cooked. To remove some of the gamey taste, I sprinkle cassava flour over the goat pieces and let it sit for a bit. Then I rinse it with water and lime juice. Goat meat is tough and requires a lot of braising to make it tender, unless you use an Instant Pot like I do in this recipe.

Servings: 4 servings
Cook Time: 55 minutes

2 lb (907 g) goat meat, cut into 2-inch (5-cm) chunks
½ cup (120 g) cassava flour
1 tbsp (15 ml) lime juice (about 1 lime)
1 tsp ground ginger
1 tsp salt
¼ tsp cayenne pepper
¼ cup (60 g) Spicy Green Seasoning (page 131)
4 tbsp (24 g) Curry Powder (page 152)
1 tbsp (5 g) Geera (page 157)
½ tsp Garam Masala (page 151)
1 tsp ground coriander
½ tsp ground mustard
1 cup (240 ml) water
¼ cup (60 ml) avocado oil
3 wiri wiri peppers or 1 habanero pepper

To Serve
Toasted Cauliflower Rice (page 136)

Into a large bowl, add the goat and generously coat with cassava flour. Let it rest for 10 minutes, then rinse thoroughly with water. Add the lime juice, mix, then rinse again. Pat dry, then add the ground ginger, salt, cayenne pepper and Spicy Green Seasoning. Marinate for 30 minutes at room temperature.

Combine the Curry Powder, Geera, Garam Masala, ground coriander, ground mustard and water in a bowl and mix together well. Set the Instant Pot to sauté. When the Instant Pot is hot, add the avocado oil. Allow the oil to get hot to the point of smoking, then add the spice mixture you prepared earlier. Cook, stirring once or twice, for about 5 minutes, or until most of the water cooks down and a thick curry paste is left. Then add the seasoned goat. Continue to cook on sauté for 10 minutes, stirring often. Add the wiri wiri peppers, seal the Instant Pot and pressure cook on high for 45 minutes.

Next, release the pressure using the rapid release function. If the liquid in the pot is too thin, set the Instant Pot to sauté and cook for an additional 5 minutes, stirring once or twice, or until the curry sauce thickens to your liking. Serve your Curry Goat over Toasted Cauliflower Rice (page 136).

NOTE: Curry Goat is typically very spicy, and this recipe is no exception. To adjust the heat, use 1 wiri wiri pepper or ⅓ of a habanero pepper, or omit them altogether.

BROWN STEW FISH

Fish stews are very popular throughout the Caribbean, but this version of fish stew is popularly called brown stew fish in Jamaica. It is typically made with whole red snapper, but I love the ease of snapper fillets, so I use those in my recipe. This stew is loaded with flavor. The fish is pan-fried, then added to a brown gravy (the brown stew) and slow cooked until the flavors infuse. To make this recipe Paleo-friendly, I used coconut aminos instead of browning.

Makes: 4 servings
Cook Time: 30 minutes

4 red snapper fillets, about 2 lb (907 g)
1 tbsp (15 ml) lemon juice (about ¼ of a lemon)
2 tbsp (30 ml) Spicy Green Seasoning (page 131)
1 tsp salt, divided
1 cup (240 ml) avocado oil or similar
½ cup (120 g) cassava flour
1 tsp garlic powder
1 tsp onion powder
½ tsp paprika
½ tsp cayenne pepper
2 tbsp (28 g) coconut oil
1 large yellow onion, sliced
5 cloves (20 g) garlic, grated
2 tomatoes, diced
1 carrot, julienned
1 red bell pepper, julienned
1 green bell pepper, julienned
2 sprigs thyme
10 allspice berries
¼ cup (60 ml) coconut aminos
2 cups (480 ml) water
3 scallions, thinly sliced, for garnish

To Serve

Toasted Cauliflower Rice (page 136)
Pan-Fried Sweet Plantains (page 139)
Avocado slices

Into a large bowl, add the fish, then sprinkle the lemon juice over the fillets. Next add the Spicy Green Seasoning and ½ teaspoon of salt. Give it a good toss to ensure that the fish is coated in the seasoning. Cover and let the fish marinate for at least 30 minutes at room temperature or no longer than overnight in the refrigerator.

Heat the avocado oil in a frying pan over medium heat. Pat the fish dry, removing any excess seasoning. Then combine the cassava flour, garlic powder, onion powder, paprika and cayenne pepper. Dredge the fish in the cassava flour mixture, shake off any excess flour, then add the fish to the hot oil. Cook for about 3 minutes, then flip and cook for 2 more minutes, or until the fish fillets are golden brown on both sides. Remove from the oil and drain on a few paper towel sheets. Set aside.

Into a skillet over medium heat, add the coconut oil, then add the sliced onion. Cook until the onion becomes a little soft, about 2 minutes, then add the garlic, tomatoes and ½ teaspoon of salt. Stir together well and continue to cook until the tomatoes soften, about 2 minutes. Add the carrot, red bell pepper, green bell pepper, thyme, allspice berries and coconut aminos. Stir into the cooked tomatoes and cook for 1 minute. Add the water.

Increase the heat to high and bring the liquid up to a boil. When it is boiling, add in the fried fish fillets you set aside earlier. Submerge the fillets, spooning some of the sauce over the fish if necessary. Then reduce the heat to medium-low and let simmer until the sauce reduces by half, about 15 minutes. Spoon some more sauce over the fillets, then add the scallions. Remove from the heat and serve with a side of Toasted Cauliflower Rice (page 136), Pan-Fried Sweet Plantains (page 139) and a few slices of avocado.

CARIBBEAN STREET FOOD

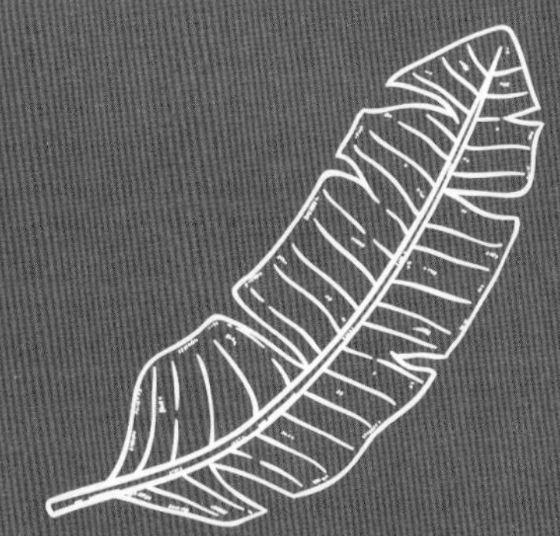

Street food is an integral part of the food culture in Caribbean countries. While it varies from country to country, some similarities can be found. Most children throughout the Caribbean buy street foods during school recess and lunch. I have fond memories of my favorite food vendors and their delicious snacks. Adults sometimes opt for a quick, inexpensive street snack for lunch or as an after-work treat. Unfortunately, most street foods are gluten-filled and not Paleo-friendly. Therefore, I wanted to tackle recreating some of my favorite Caribbean street foods in this chapter.

I start the chapter with my all-time favorite street snack, Salt Fish Cakes (page 57), also called codfish cakes and bacalaitos. These fish fritters/croquettes can be found throughout the Caribbean with little to no variation in ingredients and preparation. I was thrilled to make a Paleo version of this popular street snack, and I highly recommend you try some paired with Tamarind Chutney (page 135) or Mango and Wiri Wiri Pepper Sauce (page 147).

My other favorite recipe in this chapter is Baiganee (Eggplant Fritters) (page 61). This recipe is dear to me. It is one of my favorite things that my late grandmother Evelyn made for all her Hindu celebrations. The original recipe is made with eggplant dipped in a split pea and wheat flour batter. The thought of not ever being able to enjoy this dish again made me so sad. After testing the Paleo version, made with farine in place of split peas and cassava flour in place of wheat flour, I cried. It tasted almost exactly like my grandmother's recipe. My mom was visiting me while I tested my recipes, and she also agreed that I nailed it!

This chapter brings me so much joy, and I hope these recipes do the same for you.

SALT FISH CAKES

Salt fish cake is a Caribbean classic. Almost every Caribbean country has a version of these. They are also called salt fish fritters, codfish cakes, salt fish accra and bacalaitos. Most of the ingredients are the same from country to country and it is often seasoned flaked fish, coated in batter and deep fried. In Guyana, we don't typically make ours in a batter, but we do coat it in flour and fry it. To make this recipe Paleo-friendly, but still true to the flavors of the original dish, I keep all the traditional seasoning and replace the flour with cassava flour. I also add some farine (page 158) to the cassava mixture. Farine has the texture of cornmeal and makes a great addition to the cassava flour coating for this dish. It gives the salt fish cakes a bit of a crunchy exterior, and who doesn't like a good crunch?

Makes: 8 fish cakes
Cook Time: 6 minutes

1 lb (907 g) boneless, skinless salted Alaskan pollock or similar salted fish
8 cups (1.3 L) water, divided
4 cloves (16 g) garlic
1 small yellow onion
¼ cup (4 g) cilantro, plus additional, chopped, for garnish
3 scallions
½ lb (227 g) potatoes, cooked and crushed
½ tsp cayenne pepper
1 tsp tomato paste
1 tbsp (15 ml) coconut aminos
1 cup (240 ml) avocado oil or similar
½ cup (120 g) cassava flour
1 cup (170 g) farine (optional)
1 tsp garlic powder
1 tbsp (7 g) onion powder
Pinch of salt
Freshly cracked black pepper

To Serve

1 lemon, cut into wedges
Wiri Wiri Ranch Dressing (page 155)

Rinse the salted fish fillets with cold running water to remove as much residual salt as possible. In a saucepan over medium heat, add 4 cups (960 ml) of water and the fish fillets. Heat, uncovered, until boiling. Continue to cook uncovered for 10 minutes, then drain the water and add 4 cups (960 ml) of fresh water. Put the saucepan back over medium heat, uncovered, and bring up to a boil again. Boil for another 10 minutes, then drain the water. Rinse the fish in cold water and allow to cool completely. Flake the fish with a fork and set aside.

Add the garlic, onion, cilantro and scallions to a food processor, and blend until smooth. Combine this blended seasoning, crushed potatoes, cayenne pepper, tomato paste, coconut aminos and the flaked salt fish you set aside earlier. Mix everything together until fully combined. Shape into 8 (½-inch [1.3-cm]-thick) patties.

To cook the salt fish cakes, heat a skillet or frying pan over medium heat. When the pan is hot, add the avocado oil. Combine the cassava flour, farine (if using), garlic powder, onion powder, a pinch of salt and the cracked black pepper and mix. Coat the salt fish cakes in the seasoned cassava flour. Shake off any excess flour, then add the fish cakes to the hot oil. Cook for 3 minutes on each side, or until each side is golden brown. Remove from the heat and rest on a few sheets of paper towel. Garnish with chopped cilantro and lemon wedges. Serve with Wiri Wiri Ranch Dressing (page 155).

PEPPER SHRIMP

I didn't grow up eating shrimp or any seafood besides fish. So, I was shocked when I fell in love with shrimp later in my life. The only way I can eat shrimp is if it is well seasoned and spicy, just like this. This recipe is my take on Jamaican pepper shrimp. It is hot and spicy, so if you love seafood and heat, this is it! Typically, this dish is made with butter. I replaced the butter with ghee and use Cajun seasoning in my base so this dish is not completely authentic, but it still honors the flavor of the traditional dish. If you enjoy grass-fed butter on your Paleo journey, feel free to use that in place of the ghee in this recipe.

Makes: 4 servings
Cook Time: 8 minutes

1 lb (455 g) large head-on shrimp
¼ cup (60 ml) lemon juice (about 1 lemon), divided
1 tsp red wine vinegar
2 tbsp (30 ml) avocado oil
2 tbsp (20 g) Cajun seasoning
½ tsp smoked paprika
1 tsp annatto (achiote) powder
1 tbsp (11 g) allspice berries
6 cloves (24 g) garlic, grated
2 Scotch bonnet or habanero peppers, chopped
¼ cup (55 g) ghee
6 scallions, heads removed
4 sprigs thyme

Defrost the shrimp completely, if using frozen, then rinse clean. Pat dry. In a large bowl, add the shrimp and drizzle with the lemon juice, the red wine vinegar and avocado oil. Add the Cajun seasoning, smoked paprika, annatto powder, allspice berries, garlic and Scotch bonnet peppers. Mix together so that each shrimp is completely covered with seasoning. Let marinate for 10 minutes.

Into a skillet over medium heat, add the ghee and scallions. Add the shrimp, including the seasoning and any juices. Toss together a few times, then add the thyme, cover and let cook for 5 minutes, or until the shrimp is opaque and curls up. Remove from the heat, then remove and discard the thyme and scallions. To eat, peel the shrimp. This dish is typically enjoyed as is with no accompaniment.

BAIGANEE (EGGPLANT FRITTERS)

My childhood is calling loud and clear with this recipe. My grandmother Evelyn made delicious baiganee *(by-gun-nee), or eggplant fritters, for Hindu holidays and religious observances. This dish is typically made with sliced eggplant, dipped in a split pea batter, then fried. To make this recipe Paleo-friendly, I used farine (page 158) and cassava flour in the batter. Farine has a similar texture to the split peas traditionally used in this recipe. It was the perfect substitute. This recipe tasted so close to the traditional recipe that I was in disbelief.*

Makes: 16 fritters (4 servings)
Cook Time: 20 minutes

2 large eggplants
1¼ tsp (7 g) salt, divided
1 tbsp (7 g) onion powder
1 tsp garlic powder
1 tbsp (6 g) Curry Powder (page 152)
½ tsp Geera (page 157)
¼ tsp Garam Masala (page 151)
1 cup (240 g) cassava flour
½ cup (85 g) farine
1½ cups (360 ml) water
½ cup (110 g) coconut oil

To Serve

Tamarind Chutney (page 135)

Cut the top and bottom tips off the eggplant, then slice into round ¼-inch (6-mm)-thick slices. Sprinkle 1 teaspoon of salt over the eggplant slices, taking care to add salt to both sides of each slice. Then place in a colander. Place the colander in the sink or on a plate and let rest for 30 minutes. After 30 minutes, place the eggplant slices on a surface lined with paper towels. Blot dry with another sheet of paper towels.

In a bowl, combine the onion powder, garlic powder, Curry Powder, Geera, Garam Masala, ¼ teaspoon of salt, cassava flour and farine. Mix until fully combined. Add the water and mix until a thick but loose batter forms. Then, working in batches of six, add 1 tablespoon (15 ml) of the batter to one side of each eggplant slice, and spread it thinly to cover that side of the slice. Place the slices batter side up on a plate and set aside.

Heat the coconut oil in a skillet over medium heat. When the oil is ready, add another tablespoon (15 ml) of the batter to the unbattered side of the eggplant slices and add to the hot oil, one at a time. Work in batches, cooking about six baiganee at a time. This will prevent the oil from cooling down and allow for even cooking. Cook about 3 minutes per side, or until golden brown on each side. Then rest on paper towels, blotting with more paper towels to remove any excess oil. Repeat until all of the baiganee are battered and pan-fried. Allow to cool before serving with the Tamarind Chutney (page 135).

PLANTAIN BEEF PATTIES

Jamaican beef patties are a well-known Caribbean staple and street food. When I lived in Brooklyn, I ate my fair share of beef patties and coco bread. This recipe is heavily influenced by my love for Jamaican beef patties. They are completely Paleo and so delicious. When I first made these, I was in awe at how close to the real thing they tasted. Of course, a plantain crust will never taste exactly like a flaky pastry crust, but if you don't think too much about it these are a great Paleo substitute that celebrates the flavors of the original dish with a bit of a twist. I love using plantain as a crust in this recipe. The color of the cooked green plantains effortlessly mimics the color of the traditional Jamaican beef patty crust. The filling has all the flavor of the traditional patty recipe with the addition of cassava flour instead of wheat flour, to make it Paleo. I hope you enjoy this recipe as much as I do.

Makes: 6 patties
Cook Time: 45 minutes

- 1 tbsp (15 ml) avocado oil
- 1 small onion, diced
- 1 tsp salt, divided
- 4 cloves (16 g) garlic, grated
- 1 tbsp (6 g) Curry Powder (page 152)
- ½ lb (227 g) ground beef
- ¼ cup (60 ml) Jerk Seasoning (page 132)
- 3 tbsp (45 ml) coconut aminos
- 1 tbsp (15 g) cassava flour
- 5 cups (1.2 L) water, divided
- 2 green plantains, peeled (page 159)
- 2 egg yolks, beaten

Heat a skillet over medium heat. When the skillet is hot, add the avocado oil, the diced onion and ¼ teaspoon of salt. Cook, stirring once or twice, until the onion is soft, about 2 minutes. Add the garlic and Curry Powder and cook for an additional 2 minutes. Add the ground beef and Jerk Seasoning. Mix while continuing to cook. When most of the pink cooks off, add the coconut aminos, cassava flour and 1 cup (240 ml) of water. Continue to cook for another 2 to 3 minutes, or until the sauce thickens a little but is still loose. Remove from the heat and let cool before transferring to a food processor or blender. Blend until smooth. Set aside.

Cut the plantains into quarters, then add them to a saucepan with 4 cups (960 ml) of water and ¾ teaspoon of salt. Bring to a boil over high heat, then continue to cook until fork tender, about 15 minutes. Drain and allow to cool. Then add the cooked plantain to the food processor and process until smooth.

Preheat the oven to 375°F (190°C). Prepare a greased baking sheet.

Divide the processed plantain into six balls. One at a time, place each ball between plastic wrap and roll with a rolling pin until about ⅛ inch (3 mm) thick. Cut the round into a rectangle, then add 2 tablespoons (30 g) of the beef filling to one side of the rolled-out plantain, leaving ½ inch (1.3 cm) around the perimeter. Fold the other side of the plantain over the filling and press the edges together to seal. Use a fork to crimp the edges. Repeat with the rest of the plantain balls.

Add the plantain beef patties to the prepared baking sheet, and brush each patty with the beaten egg yolks. Bake at 375°F (190°C) for 30 minutes, or until the tops get brown and a bit glossy. Remove from the oven and allow to cool before serving.

NOTE: These plantain beef patties are best eaten fresh. They reheat well in the microwave but may get a bit stiff when they start to cool down after reheating. Any remaining meat filling can be frozen for future use.

CASSAVA CHICKEN PATTIES

A chicken patty is a popular Guyanese turnover or savory hand pie. They are traditionally made with seasoned ground chicken in a pastry crust. They are very similar to chicken empanadas. When I started exploring grain-free substitutions for patties, I thought about how pliable cassava is when crushed, and to my surprise it works really well as a "dough." Just boiling and crushing the cassava makes it moldable. Just be careful not to overcook the cassava or it will be too mushy to work with. Besides using cassava as the crust in this recipe, I also substituted soy sauce and sugar with coconut aminos in the filling, making this a truly delicious substitute for real-deal chicken patties. You could also easily use other types of ground meat in this recipe to make different variations. Try ground beef, pork or turkey to mix it up, if you like.

Makes: 8 patties (4 servings)
Cook Time: 45 minutes

2 lb (907 g) cassava, peeled and cut into 2-inch (5-cm) pieces (page 158)
1 tsp kosher salt, plus more to taste if needed
6 cups (1.4 L) water
2 tbsp (30 ml) avocado oil or similar
½ lb (227 g) ground chicken
2 tbsp (30 ml) Spicy Green Seasoning (page 131)
1 tbsp (15 ml) coconut aminos
½ red bell pepper, diced
½ green bell pepper, diced
4 scallions, thinly sliced
3 egg yolks, beaten

Into a saucepan, add the cassava, kosher salt, and enough water to cover the cassava pieces completely (about 6 cups [1.4 L] of water). Bring to a boil over medium heat and cook uncovered until the cassava is fork tender, about 15 minutes. Then drain and allow to cool completely.

Remove the inner fibrous veins from the cassava pieces, then, using a fork or a potato masher, crush the cassava until smooth. Set aside. You can also use a potato ricer for this step if you have one.

Heat the avocado oil in a skillet over medium heat. Add the ground chicken, the Spicy Green Seasoning and coconut aminos. Stir often to break up any ground chicken chunks that may form during cooking. Cook until all the visible pink of the chicken is gone, about 5 minutes. Add the red and green bell peppers and mix. Continue to cook for 1 to 2 minutes, then finish off with the scallions. Taste and add salt if needed. Allow to cool completely.

Preheat the oven to 350°F (175°C). Prepare a greased baking sheet.

Divide the mashed cassava into 16 pieces and roll them into balls. One at a time, place each ball between plastic wrap and, using a rolling pin, roll them into flat disks. If you have a tortilla press, you can use it for this step.

Place one disk on a flat surface, then add the chicken filling to the center, leaving ¼ inch (0.6 cm) around the edge of the disk. Brush the edges with some water, then top with another disk. Dip a fork in some water and press it down on all the edges to seal the disks together, making a pattern around the edges of the hand pie. Repeat these steps until all your cassava chicken patties are formed.

Brush the top of each hand pie with the beaten egg yolk. Using the fork, poke a few holes in the top of each pie.

Place the hand pies on the prepared baking sheet and bake for 30 minutes, or until the crust becomes brown. Remove from the oven and allow to cool before enjoying.

PLANTAIN STRIPS AND CUCUMBER SOUR

Plantain chips and mango sour (what we call mango chutney in Guyana) is a popular schoolyard and street snack that I still enjoy as an adult. It is one of those recipes that is naturally Paleo and needs no adjustment. Instead of mangoes, I paired my plantain strips with cucumber sour that is also naturally Paleo, because it is easy to make and because unlike mangoes, cucumbers are available in every season.

Makes: 4 servings
Cook Time: 20 minutes

Plantain Strips

4 large green plantains with no yellow spots, peeled (page 159)

¼ cup (60 ml) avocado oil or similar

1 tsp coarse salt

Cucumber Sour

1 large cucumber, peeled and diced

1 cup (240 ml) water

½ tsp Geera (page 157)

1 tsp coarse salt

3 cloves (12 g) garlic

2 scallions

2 wiri wiri peppers or other chili peppers

1 tsp distilled white vinegar

To make the plantain strips, preheat the oven to 350°F (175°C). Prepare a sheet pan lined with parchment paper.

Using a mandoline slicer, slice the plantains into ⅛-inch (3-mm) strips. Add the strips to a bowl and drizzle with avocado oil. Gently toss to ensure both sides of each strip are coated in oil.

Place the plantains in a single layer on the prepared sheet pan. Bake for 15 minutes, or until the edges start to brown. Remove from the oven and sprinkle with the coarse salt. Allow to cool completely. The strips will crisp up after cooling.

To make the cucumber sour, add the cucumbers to a saucepan with the water, Geera, salt, garlic, scallions and wiri wiri peppers. Bring to a boil over medium heat. Continue to cook until the cucumbers are tender, about 3 minutes, then remove from the heat and add the white vinegar. Allow to cool, then add to a blender or food processor and blend into a sauce similar to salsa in consistency. This should take less than a minute.

Allow to cool completely before serving with the plantain chips. Enjoy this dish by scooping up bits of the chutney with the plantain strips. It is essentially my Caribbean version of chips and salsa.

CASSAVA BALLS

Cassava balls are a popular Guyanese schoolyard snack and street food. They are served with a spicy chutney made either with green mangoes or tamarind. Traditionally, the cassava mixture is coated in a batter made with flour or it is simply dusted with flour, then deep-fried. To make this recipe Paleo, I substituted the wheat flour for cassava flour and shallow-fried the cassava balls. These gluten- and grain-free cassava balls taste as authentic as the traditional recipe. Pair them with my Tamarind Chutney (page 135) for a savory, sweet and spicy bite of goodness.

Makes: 10–12 cassava balls
Cook Time: 25 minutes

1½ lb (670 g) cassava, peeled and cut into 2-inch (5-cm) pieces (page 158)
1½ tsp (10 g) salt, plus a pinch, divided
4 cups (960 ml) water, plus more if needed
2 eggs, beaten
2 cups (480 g) cassava flour, divided
4 cloves (16 g) garlic, grated
3 scallions, thinly sliced
Freshly cracked black pepper
2 cups (480 ml) avocado oil
½ tsp garlic powder
½ tsp onion power

To Serve

Tamarind Chutney (page 135)

Into a saucepan, add the cassava, 1 teaspoon of salt and water, adding more if needed to cover the cassava. Over high heat, uncovered, bring the mixture to a boil. Continue to cook uncovered for 15 minutes, or until the cassava is soft and can be easily crushed with a fork. Remove from the heat and drain.

In a bowl, combine the cooked cassava, a pinch of salt, the beaten eggs, 1 cup (240 g) of the cassava flour, garlic, scallions and cracked black pepper. Mix until fully combined. Form the cassava mixture into 10 to 12 balls. I love using a 1½-tablespoon (3-cm diameter) cookie scoop for this, but you may also spoon about 2 heaping tablespoons (30 g) of the mixture into the palm of your hand (rub a bit of avocado oil on your palms first). Then roll the mixture between your palms to form a ball. Repeat until you've made all the cassava balls.

Heat the oil in a frying pan over medium heat. On a small plate or in a bowl, combine the remaining 1 cup (240 g) of cassava flour, remaining salt, garlic powder and onion powder. Roll each cassava ball into the seasoned cassava flour and set aside. When the oil is ready, working in two batches, add the cassava balls to the hot oil. Fry on each side until golden brown, about 1 minute on each side. Rotate the cassava ball in the oil, so that all the sides fry up evenly.

Remove the cassava balls from the oil and drain on a few sheets of paper towel to remove excess oil. Then serve with some delicious Tamarind Chutney (page 135).

POTATO EGG BALLS

Egg balls are a popular Guyanese street food. They look very much like Scotch eggs, but instead of a boiled egg encased in meat, it is a boiled egg typically encased in cassava and sometimes encased in potato. Cassava egg balls will always be one of my top five favorite Guyanese street snacks and is a top recipe on my blog, metemgee.com. This Potato Egg Ball recipe replaces the cassava from the original recipe with creamy white potatoes. If white potatoes are not part of your Paleo diet, feel free to use sweet potatoes.

Makes: 4 egg balls
Cook Time: 20 minutes

1½ lb (670 g) potatoes
4 cups (960 ml) water
1½ tsp (10 g) salt, plus a pinch, divided
1 tbsp (11 g) onion powder, divided
4 cloves (16 g) garlic, grated
3 scallions, thinly sliced
2 wiri wiri peppers, deseeded and deveined, finely chopped
4 eggs, boiled for 6–8 minutes, peeled
2 cups (480 ml) avocado oil
½ cup (120 g) cassava flour
½ tsp garlic powder
¼ tsp turmeric

To Serve

Tamarind Chutney (page 135) or Cucumber Sour (page 65)

To a large stockpot over high heat, add the whole potatoes, water and 1 teaspoon of salt. Cover and bring to a boil. Continue to cook with the lid slightly ajar for about 15 minutes, or until the potatoes are fork tender, then drain. Allow the potatoes to cool completely, then peel and crush.

To the crushed potatoes, add a pinch of salt, 1 teaspoon of onion powder, garlic and scallions. Add the wiri wiri peppers. Mix until everything is fully combined.

Separate the potato mixture into four balls. Flatten each ball in the palm of your hand, then place a boiled egg in the center. Wrap the potato mixture around the egg until the egg is completely covered. Roll the covered egg between your palms to smoothen.

Heat the avocado oil in a skillet over medium heat. Then combine the cassava flour, 2 teaspoons (7 g) of onion powder, garlic powder, turmeric and a pinch of salt. Roll each egg ball into the mixture until it is fully covered. Brush off any excess flour, then add the egg balls to the hot oil and fry until golden brown, about 3 minutes, turning as often as needed for even browning. Remove from the heat and drain on a few sheets of paper towels. Serve hot with some Tamarind Chutney (page 135) or Cucumber Sour (page 65).

SPICY FISH SANDWICH

Fish and bake is my favorite type of fish sandwich. You just can't say no to fried fish stuffed into sweet bakes (a Caribbean fried dough). In this version, I replaced the bakes with twice-fried smashed plantains to make this recipe Paleo-friendly. Top this sandwich off with a spicy mango slaw and all the flavors come together in one crunchy bite. It takes a bit of time to prep each of the components, but it is so worth it.

Makes: 4 sandwiches
Cook Time: 30 minutes

Fish

4 red snapper fillets, about 2 lb (907 g)

1 tbsp (15 ml) lemon juice (about ¼ of a lemon)

2 tbsp (30 ml) Spicy Green Seasoning (page 131)

1 tsp salt

½ cup (120 g) cassava flour

1 tsp garlic powder

1 tsp onion powder

½ tsp paprika

½ tsp cayenne pepper

Plantains

2 green plantains with a hint of yellow, peeled (page 159)

1 cup (240 ml) avocado oil or similar

Spicy Mango Slaw

1 cup (70 g) shredded cabbage

1 carrot, shredded

1 mango, shredded

¼ cup (4 g) cilantro, finely chopped

2 scallions, sliced diagonally

½ tsp salt

2 tbsp (30 ml) Wiri Wiri Ranch Dressing (page 155) or other ranch dressing

To Serve

Paleo-friendly ketchup

Mango and Wiri Wiri Pepper Sauce (page 147)

Avocado slices

To marinate the fish, into a bowl, add the fish, lemon juice, Spicy Green Seasoning and salt. Toss to coat the fish with the seasoning. Cover and let marinate for at least 30 minutes or overnight in the refrigerator if time allows. If marinating overnight, let the fish rest at room temperature for at least 1 hour before cooking.

To make the plantains, cut the plantains into halves, then cut each half in half again lengthwise.

Heat the avocado oil in a skillet over medium heat. Prepare a sheet of parchment paper and an object with a flat base, like a bowl, mug or Mason jar, for smashing the fried plantains.

Add the plantains to the hot oil and cook for 3 minutes on each side, or until the plantains cook all the way through. Remove from the heat. Place between parchment paper and smash until flattened, using your object with a flat base. Return to the hot oil and fry for 1 minute on each side, then drain on a few sheets of paper towels.

To cook the fish, keep the oil from frying the plantains hot. Combine the cassava flour, garlic powder, onion powder, paprika and cayenne pepper. Pat the fish dry, removing any excess seasoning. Cover the fish with the cassava flour mixture, flipping over and dusting with the cassava flour if necessary. Shake off any excess flour, then add the fish to the hot oil used to fry the plantains. Cook for about 3 minutes on each side, or until the fish fillets are golden brown. Then remove from the oil and drain on a few paper towel sheets.

To make the mango slaw, combine the cabbage, carrot, mango, cilantro and scallions in a bowl, and sprinkle with the salt. Drizzle with the Wiri Wiri Ranch or other ranch dressing and mix well.

Assemble your sandwich by placing a fried plantain on a plate. Add some Paleo-friendly ketchup and Mango and Wiri Wiri Pepper Sauce (page 147). Then add a fried fish fillet and top it with some spicy mango slaw and a few avocado slices. Top with another piece of fried plantain and your Spicy Fish Sandwich is ready.

STRIPPED CHICKEN FRIED RICE

A good one-pot dish can save you when you are in a pinch. This one does not disappoint. It is my Paleo version of Guyanese stripped chicken fried rice. You can use leftover chicken breast or any meat from a store-bought rotisserie chicken for this recipe. Just be careful to read the ingredients on the chicken if using store-bought to ensure there are no additives that aren't compatible with the Paleo diet or how you eat.

Makes: 4 servings
Cook Time: 15 minutes

- 2 tbsp (30 ml) avocado oil
- 1 tbsp (15 ml) sesame oil
- 1 small yellow onion, diced
- 1 tsp coarse salt, plus a pinch, divided
- 4 cloves (16 g) garlic, grated
- 1 red bell pepper, diced
- ½ cup (60 g) Chinese long beans, thinly sliced, or green beans, peas or asparagus
- 1 large carrot, diced
- 1 tsp Chinese five spice
- ¼ cup (60 ml) coconut aminos
- 1 lb (454 g) chicken breasts, cooked and shredded
- 1 lb (454 g) Toasted Cauliflower Rice (page 136)

Pickled Cucumbers (page 144)

Into a skillet or wok over high heat, add the avocado and sesame oils. Add the onion and a pinch of coarse salt and cook until the onion starts to brown, about 1 minute. Add the garlic, bell pepper, Chinese long beans, carrot, Chinese five spice and coconut aminos. Stir to combine and continue to cook over high heat for another 5 minutes, stirring often for even cooking.

Add the cooked chicken breasts, remaining salt and the Toasted Cauliflower Rice. Toss to combine and continue to cook for another 3 minutes, stirring continuously to warm up the rice and the chicken. Remove from the heat and serve hot with a side of Pickled Cucumbers (page 144).

FRUIT CHOW

Imagine a really tasty fruit salad with a bit of acid and some heat. Chow is more of a quick pickle than a fruit salad, but you get the idea. I didn't grow up calling this dish chow. Chow is more of a Trinidadian name, but it has grown on me. In Guyana, we simply say whatever fruit you are eating paired with salt and pepper. For example: mango and salt and pepper. If vinegar was added and it was stored in a bottle overnight or for a few days, it was simply pickle mango. You can eat this dish on its own or as a topping for protein. It works really well on fish, especially fish tacos.

Makes: 4 servings
Prep Time: 10 minutes

1 mango with firm yellow flesh, peeled and cut into chunks

1 heaping cup (200 g) papaya, seeds removed, cut into chunks

1 heaping cup (200 g) pineapple, cut into chunks

1 tbsp (15 ml) lime juice (about 1 lime)

Zest of 1 lime

1 tsp coarse salt

2 wiri wiri peppers or ½ habanero pepper, minced

6 culantro leaves, or a handful of cilantro, finely chopped

In a bowl, combine the mango, papaya, pineapple, lime juice, lime zest, coarse salt, wiri wiri peppers and culantro and mix well. Let rest for 10 to 15 minutes to allow the flavors to come together. Serve at room temperature or chilled.

FLAVAH-FUL SIDES

Rice is a staple side dish in Caribbean cooking. Most meals are protein, veggies and a side of rice. I missed rice the most when I first became Paleo, until I started exploring all the amazing root and other vegetables that I could use to fill my plate. Mastering the art of cooking riced cauliflower was one of those victories I didn't think I needed, and my Seasoned Cauliflower Rice is simple and kid-approved. My three children still don't know that it is not real rice! My love for plantains deepened when I made plantain salad, shared in this chapter as my Deviled Eggs Plantain Salad (page 77). Making Cassava Choka (page 85) was a great, new and delicious way to incorporate a root vegetable I love deeply into my Paleo lifestyle. Using these vegetables in new ways gave me so much joy, and I imagined this is how my ancestors ate before the introduction of grains into their diets.

Needing to expand my Paleo side dish options also led to testing recipes with cassava farine as a grain replacement. Cassava farine, just called farine in Guyana and other Caribbean countries, is short for Farinha de Mandioca. It is made from dried cassava pulp. Its texture is very similar to almond or cornmeal and if I had to describe it to someone unfamiliar with it, I would describe it as a type of cassava meal. In Guyana, it is made almost exclusively by Ameridians, our indigenous people. It can be found in African markets and online at Amazon.com.

I get excited when I talk about farine in Paleo cooking. It offers something riced veggies cannot: a true grain-like texture. And you can use it in recipes the way you would cornmeal, couscous and quinoa. It is also nut-free and great for those who cannot have almond meal. Farine is fully cooked and can be eaten as is, on top of stews like a garnish, or reconstituted with hot water or broth. I'm giddy with excitement for you to try my Cassava Couscous Salad made with farine (page 78) or my Nutty Farine Pilaf (page 82). I am also just happy to introduce this ingredient to you (if you are not familiar with it) and hopefully you can use it in your Paleo cooking.

DEVILED EGGS PLANTAIN SALAD

With slightly sweet yellow plantains, paired with all the goodness of deviled eggs and bacon, this side dish is sure to become a favorite. Choose plantains that are yellow with as few black spots as possible. In Guyana, we call these "turning plantains" because they are just starting to turn ripe. They are the best for this dish, because they are starchy like potatoes but a bit soft and a little sweet.

Makes: 4 servings
Cook Time: 20 minutes

- 2 lb (907 g) firm yellow plantains, peeled (page 159)
- 4 cups (960 ml) water
- 1 tsp salt, divided
- 2 cloves (8 g) garlic
- 6 hard-boiled eggs, peeled
- 1 cup (240 ml) Paleo-friendly mayo, divided
- 1 tsp spicy brown mustard
- 1 tsp smoked paprika, divided
- Freshly cracked black pepper
- ½ tsp garlic powder
- ½ red onion, diced
- ¼ cup (15 g) Italian parsley, chopped
- 4 strips Paleo-friendly bacon, cooked until crispy

Cut the plantains into bite-size cubes and add to a saucepan with the water, ¾ teaspoon of salt and garlic. Bring to a boil over high heat and continue to cook until fork tender, about 10 minutes. Drain and set aside in a bowl.

Slice the hard-boiled eggs in half. Scoop out the yolks and place them in a small bowl. Chop up the egg whites and add them to the bowl with the plantains. Into the bowl with the egg yolks, add ½ cup (120 ml) of mayo, spicy brown mustard, ½ teaspoon of smoked paprika, ¼ teaspoon of salt, freshly cracked pepper and garlic powder. Mash the yolks and mix to make a paste.

Add the egg yolk mixture to the plantains and egg whites along with ½ cup (120 ml) of mayo, the red onion and parsley. Toss to combine until all the plantains are covered in the creamy mixture. Crumble the bacon on top. Chill in the refrigerator or serve at room temperature.

CASSAVA COUSCOUS SALAD

Although this recipe is called cassava couscous, it is made with farine and not couscous. Farine has a fine, couscous-like texture, which makes it a perfect couscous substitute. I love the brightness of this dish. The freshness of the red onions, tomatoes, mangoes and basil feels like a bit of the Caribbean in every bite. If you are missing couscous or quinoa salads in your Paleo diet, please give this recipe a try. You can buy farine from Amazon by searching for "gari" or "garri." It comes in two varieties, white and yellow. The yellow one has palm oil added to it. Stick to the white one if you do not use palm oil as part of your diet.

Makes: 4 servings
Cook Time: 10 minutes

1 cup (240 ml) chicken or vegetable broth
½ tsp kosher salt
1 cup (170 g) farine
½ red onion, diced
1 heaping cup (185 g) plum tomatoes, halved
2 Hass avocados, diced or 1 cup (150 g) diced tropical avocados
1 cup (165 g) diced yellow mango
10 basil leaves, finely chopped
1 tbsp (15 ml) coconut aminos
Juice and zest of 1 lemon
Pinch of freshly cracked black pepper
Coarse salt to taste

In a saucepan over medium heat, bring the chicken broth and kosher salt to a boil. Then add the farine and mix well. Remove from the heat, cover and let sit until the farine is fully reconstituted, about 5 minutes.

In a large bowl, combine the red onion, tomatoes, avocados, mangoes, basil, coconut aminos, lemon juice and zest. Mix until fully combined. Add the reconstituted farine, cracked black pepper and additional coarse salt if needed. Mix. You may serve chilled or at room temperature.

ISLAND PASTA

This dish is influenced by a popular Caribbean dish called Rasta pasta. I don't know how the original version of this dish came about. It is typically penne pasta in an alfredo sauce, topped with some kind of jerk protein. The dish itself is delicious but the name is very controversial because Rastafarians (shortened here to Rasta) wouldn't typically eat pasta with dairy, let alone topped with meat, since they are vegans. I believe the name comes from the red, yellow and green bell peppers used in the dish, the signature Rastafarian colors. My version of this dish is completely vegan, Rasta- and Paleo-friendly and just as tasty as the original. Instead of pasta, I use roasted spaghetti squash as my "noodles" and the creamy base is completely dairy- and gluten-free. It is a great vegetable-forward dish and can be eaten without protein. However, if you'd like to try this alongside a main dish, it pairs really well with Oven-Braised Oxtail (page 23).

Makes: 4–6 servings
Cook Time: 50 minutes

2 spaghetti squash, halved lengthwise, guts and seeds removed
¼ cup (60 ml) extra virgin olive oil
1½ tsp (10 g) coarse salt, divided
¼ cup (55 g) ghee or coconut oil, divided
1 yellow bell pepper, julienned
1 red bell pepper, julienned
1 green bell pepper, julienned
2 tbsp (30 g) cassava flour
2 cups (480 ml) full-fat coconut milk
1 tbsp (7 g) onion powder
1 tsp garlic powder
¼ tsp freshly cracked black pepper
2 tbsp (10 g) nutritional yeast
½ tsp smoked paprika
¼ cup (15 g) parsley, chopped

To Serve

Oven-Braised Oxtail (page 23)

Preheat the oven to 450°F (230°C). Prepare a sheet pan lined with parchment paper.

Rub the flesh side of each spaghetti squash half with 1 tablespoon (15 ml) of extra virgin olive oil and about ¼ tsp teaspoon of the coarse salt. Place flesh side down on the prepared pan. Roast for 35 minutes, or until the skin can be easily pierced with a fork. Allow the squash to cool, then scoop the strands from the skin and set aside. If the shells remain intact, you may save them to use as a serving dish for the pasta.

Heat a skillet over medium-high heat. Add 2 tablespoons (28 g) of the ghee. When the ghee is hot, add the yellow, red and green bell peppers and cook for 1 minute, stirring often. Remove the bell peppers from the skillet and set aside. Turn the heat down to medium. Add the cassava flour and remaining ghee to the skillet and mix. Whisk in the coconut milk, onion powder, garlic powder, ½ teaspoon of salt, cracked black pepper, nutritional yeast and smoked paprika. Continue to cook over medium heat, whisking continuously, until the sauce thickens. This should take 3 to 5 minutes.

Add the roasted spaghetti squash, cooked bell peppers and parsley to the sauce. Toss and serve hot, in the spaghetti squash shells, if using. Try it with some Oven-Braised Oxtail (see page 23).

NUTTY FARINE PILAF

If you've ever tried any dishes with quinoa and nuts, you'll notice some similarities in this recipe. This Nutty Farine Pliaf is a Paleo remix of a quinoa dish I enjoyed before going Paleo. It is the perfect grain-free holiday or anytime-you-want dish with a bit of texture and crunch. I just love farine with warm spices, nuts, dried fruit and pomegranate. To keep this dish Paleo, be sure to check the labels on your dried fruits. Only choose dried fruit sweetened with fruit juices.

Servings: 4
Cook Time: 20 minutes

2 cups (480 ml) chicken or vegetable broth
1 cup (170 g) farine
¼ cup (55 g) ghee
1 shallot, diced
1 tsp fennel seeds
1 tsp whole cloves
2 cinnamon sticks
3 cardamom pods
½ cup (54 g) almond slices
1 cup (145 g) raisins
½ cup (60 g) dried cranberries or other dried fruits
½ cup (75 g) pomegranate seeds
½ cup (8 g) cilantro, chopped

In a small saucepan, warm the chicken broth over medium heat. Add the farine to a bowl, then pour the warm broth over the farine. Mix well, cover and let the farine reconstitute, about 5 minutes. When it is ready, the farine will look loose and a lot like tiny couscous.

Heat a skillet over medium heat. When it is hot, add the ghee, followed by the diced shallot. Cook, stirring once or twice, until the shallots are slightly translucent. Then add the fennel seeds, cloves, cinnamon sticks and cardamom pods.

Continue to cook over medium heat until the spices look a bit dark and toasted, about 2 minutes. Then add the almond slices, raisins and cranberries. Mix well, then reduce the heat to low and allow the dried fruit to plump up a bit. Remove from the heat.

Add the reconstituted farine, the pomegranate seeds and the chopped cilantro and gently toss together. Serve warm.

NOTE: Farine is a type of cassava meal (page 110). You can find it in African markets or on Amazon as "gari" or "garri." It has the perfect texture for dishes that typically include quinoa, like this one.

CASSAVA CHOKA

I grew up eating potato choka: white potatoes boiled, mashed and seasoned. This is my Paleo version of that dish, using nutrient-dense cassava instead of white potatoes. The flavor of this dish is amazing. Mashed cassava topped with seasoned buttery, garlicky ghee and scallions goes really well with almost any protein but I recommend pairing it with my Bhunjal Lamb Chops (page 44) for an exceptional meal. Or eat it on its own, cross-legged on the floor with a spoon, like I do. Just remember to share.

Servings: 4
Cook Time: 25 minutes

2 lb (907 g) cassava, peeled and cut into 2-inch (5-cm) pieces (page 158)
1¼ tsp (8 g) coarse salt, divided
6 cups (1.5 L) water, plus more if needed
½ cup (110 g) ghee or avocado oil
8 cloves (32 g) garlic, sliced
4 scallions, thinly sliced
2 wiri wiri peppers, finely chopped, seeds and veins removed
Freshly cracked black pepper

To Serve

Bhunjal Lamb Chops (page 44)
Cooked Paleo-friendly bacon
Eggs, cooked to your preference

Into a saucepan, add the cassava, 1 teaspoon of coarse salt and water, adding more if needed to cover the cassava. Bring to a boil over high heat. Cook, uncovered, for 20 minutes, or until the cassava is fork tender and a bit mushy. It will look a bit translucent. Drain, reserving ½ cup (120 ml) of the liquid.

Transfer the cassava to a large mixing bowl. Remove the stringy center vein from the cassava, then crush with a potato masher or fork. For a really smooth and creamy mashed cassava, you may use a potato ricer, if you have one.

Warm a skillet over medium heat. Add the ghee. When the ghee is hot, add the garlic and cook until light brown, about 3 minutes. Then add the scallions and wiri wiri peppers and cook for another minute. Pour the hot ghee over the cassava, followed by the cracked black pepper and ¼ teaspoon of salt, and mix well. Serve with Bhunjal Lamb Chops (page 44) or bacon and eggs for breakfast.

STRING BEANS IN COCONUT MILK

One thing I can tell you about Caribbean people is that if any vegetable looks remotely similar to a vegetable that we know and love, we will make it work in a recipe. In Guyana, we use Chinese long beans in our cooking. When I can't source Chinese long beans, I substitute them with string beans, like I did with this recipe that is now a hit in my home. Serve this as a side dish with Classic Chicken Stew (page 47) and Toasted Cauliflower Rice (page 136) and thank me later.

Makes: 4 servings
Cook Time: 20 minutes

2 tbsp (28 g) coconut oil
1 small yellow onion, diced
4 tomatoes, diced
5 cloves (20 g) garlic, grated
1 tsp salt, plus a pinch, divided
1 lb (454 g) string beans, cut in halves
1½ cups (360 ml) coconut milk, divided
1 cup (240 ml) water

To Serve

Classic Chicken Stew (page 47)
Toasted Cauliflower Rice (page 136)

Warm a skillet over high heat. Add the coconut oil, then the onion. Cook the onion until soft, about 2 minutes, stirring once or twice. Add the tomatoes, garlic and a pinch of salt. Toss together. Continue to cook over high heat for another 2 to 3 minutes, or until the tomatoes start to soften, then add the string beans and the remaining salt. Cook, stirring often to avoid burning. Continue to cook until the beans start to brown a little, about 5 minutes.

Add 1 cup (240 ml) of coconut milk and water and continue to cook over high heat until the liquids cook down, 10 minutes. Add ½ cup (120 ml) of coconut milk and cook for an additional minute or two. Remove from the heat and serve with some Classic Chicken Stew (page 47) and Toasted Cauliflower Rice (page 136).

SEASONED CAULI-FLOWER RICE

Seasoned Cauliflower Rice is one of the easiest, yet most delicious rice substitute side dishes you can make! It is so flavorful and comes together within minutes. I love using frozen riced cauliflower for this dish, because it has more cauliflower stalks than florets and the texture is closer to real rice versus fresh riced cauliflower.

Makes: 4 servings
Cook Time: 10 minutes

20 oz (547 g) frozen riced cauliflower, completely defrosted
1 tsp coarse salt, plus a pinch, divided
3 tbsp (45 ml) olive oil or similiar
1 shallot, diced
1 red bell pepper, diced
4 cloves (16 g) garlic, grated
½ cup (30 g) Italian parsley, finely chopped

Heat a skillet over high heat until it is almost to the point of smoking (page 51). Then add the riced cauliflower in an even layer. Cook for 2 to 3 minutes, or until all the liquid cooks off and the rice starts to brown. Sprinkle with ½ teaspoon of coarse salt, then toss the rice. Continue to cook for another 1 to 2 minutes, or until most of the rice is brown and toasted. Remove from the heat and add the rice to a large serving bowl.

Return the skillet to medium heat, then add the olive oil. Add the shallot and a pinch of salt. Cook, stirring often until the shallots become translucent. Add the bell pepper, garlic and ½ teaspoon of salt and mix to combine. Cook for another minute.

To serve, you can mix the seasoning into the toasted cauliflower rice, then serve, or you can mix the seasoning in tableside. Top with the parsley.

SAUTÉED CALLALOO

Callaloo is a green leafy vegetable similar to spinach. The callaloo used in this recipe is Jamaican callaloo or Chinese spinach. I get mine from my local Asian market. If you can't source this type of callaloo, fresh leafy spinach also works in this recipe. This is one of those recipes that needed no adjustments to be Paleo. I added in a tiny bit of coconut aminos, but the recipe is just as delicious without it. It is a quick and easy way to add some veggies to a meal.

Makes: 4 servings
Cook Time: 20 minutes

¼ cup (55 g) coconut oil
1 yellow onion, diced
½ tsp salt
4 cloves (16 g) garlic, grated
4 tomatoes, diced
1 lb (907 g) Jamaican callaloo or Chinese spinach (Amaranth), chopped (see Note)
1 tbsp (15 ml) coconut aminos (optional)

To Serve

Toasted Cauliflower Rice (page 136)
Potato Roti (page 105)

Heat a large skillet over high heat. When the skillet is hot, add the coconut oil. Add the onion and salt. Cook, stirring often, until the onion starts to brown. Then add the garlic and tomatoes. Continue to cook over high heat until the tomatoes are mushy, about 5 minutes.

Add the callaloo and coconut aminos (if using) and toss gently to combine. You may also do this in small batches. Cover, reduce the heat to medium, and let the callaloo steam until it becomes dark brown in color, 10 minutes. Then increase the heat to high and continue to cook uncovered until all the liquids cook down. Continue to cook for 1 minute, stirring often, then remove from the heat. I love pairing my sauéed callaloo with Toasted Cauliflower Rice (page 136) or Potato Roti (page 105) for a simple and delicious meal.

NOTE: Steep your callaloo bunches in a large bowl or clean sink full of water. Rinse under fresh running water to remove any sand or debris. Inspect each bunch and remove dead leaves or any leaves with lots of holes. Using a paring knife, strip away as much of the thin membrane from the thicker stalk as possible. Chop the thick stalk into 1-inch (2.5-cm) pieces, then rough chop the leaves and smaller leafy stalks.

CARIBBEAN YELLOW RICE

Yellow rice is also called saffron rice in the Caribbean and is not to be confused with the spice saffron, which is added to dishes like paella. This is a delicious side dish with bright flavors from the turmeric and the Basic Green Seasoning (page 131). To make this dish Paleo, I used rice cauliflower instead of real rice, but all the flavors are exactly as the original dish. This is another dish that I serve often and my children don't know it is not real rice. It pairs well with any protein but my favorite way to serve it is as a side when I make Saucy Baked Chicken (page 29) for Sunday dinners.

Makes: 4 servings
Cook Time: 15 minutes

2 tbsp (28 g) coconut oil
¼ cup (60 ml) Basic Green Seasoning (page 131)
20 oz (547 g) frozen riced cauliflower, completely defrosted
1½ tsp (10 g) kosher salt
¼ tsp turmeric
2 scallions, thinly sliced

To Serve

Saucy Baked Chicken (page 29)

In a hot skillet over medium heat, add the coconut oil. Add the Basic Green Seasoning followed by the riced cauliflower. Mix well, then let cook untouched for 5 minutes, or until the cauliflower starts to brown a little. Continue to cook over medium heat, stirring often, until most of the riced cauliflower is brown.

Add the kosher salt, turmeric and scallions. Toss to combine. Continue to cook for another 2 to 3 minutes. Remove from the heat and serve alongside some Saucy Baked Chicken (page 29).

GRILLED OKRA CHOKA

Okra, also called okro (ochro) in the Caribbean is one of those vegetables that you either love or hate. I love it, but only when it is cooked dry and crisp, not slimy. One of the easiest ways to achieve that delicious crisp okra that I love so much is to grill it over high heat. This makes a great side dish and pairs well with fish or shrimp.

Makes: 4 servings
Cook Time: 20 minutes

2 lb (907 g) whole okras, washed, patted dry, tops and tips removed, and cut into lengthwise halves

2 tbsp (30 ml) avocado oil or similar, divided

2 medium tomatoes, cut into wedges

1 red onion, sliced

4 cloves (16 g) garlic, sliced

1 tsp salt

To Serve

Jerk Chicken Under a Brick (page 16)

Brown Stew Fish (page 53)

Preheat the grill to 400°F (205°C). Drizzle the okra with 1 tablespoon (15 ml) of oil. Add the okra to a grill basket or a cast iron skillet and grill for 15 minutes, tossing once or twice. The okra should have a bit of char and look slightly dehydrated. Place in a bowl and set aside.

Grease the grill grate, then add the tomatoes. Grill for 3 minutes on each side, or until the tomato wedges have grill marks. Add the grilled tomato wedges to the okra.

Add a skillet to medium heat. When the skillet is hot, add 1 tablespoon (15 ml) of oil followed by the onion and garlic. Cook until the garlic is golden brown, then remove from the heat. Pour over the grilled okra and tomatoes. Sprinkle with salt and toss together. This is a great side for my Jerk Chicken Under a Brick (page 16) or Brown Stew Fish (page 53).

CARIBBEAN BREAKFAST

Breakfast is the most important meal of the day. Growing up in Guyana, my breakfast often consisted of a vegetable dish and roti or fried bakes. My mom woke up ahead of us to cook breakfast and pack up leftovers for lunch. On weekends, we ate eggs and sausage with plantains or sautéed salted fish and fried bakes. It was also not uncommon to fry up some "egg and rice" for a late breakfast (brunch) on a busy Sunday morning. I still do this, but now I make Egg and Cauliflower Rice (page 106).

Now that I am Paleo, my breakfast looks a little different than back then, but with some of the same elements. I love making Plantain and Bacon Fritters (page 100) as part of my breakfast meal prep and enjoying them throughout the week. They are simple to make in a batch and reheat like a dream. I still eat roti for breakfast and my Paleo Potato Roti (page 105) is delicious on its own, but even better when paired with Oven-Roasted Baigan and Shrimp Choka (page 101).

When I miss a hot cup of porridge, I whip up some Farine Porridge (page 110) and top it with some freshly grated nutmeg, maple syrup and fruit. Cozying up to the warmth of the farine and the spices makes me fulfilled and nourished.

SALMON AND CREAMY FARINE POLENTA

Make this when you need a quick brunch dish that is as impressive as it is delicious: saucy salmon on a bowl of creamy farine cooked to mimic polenta. The farine looks and tastes so much like polenta that your brain won't know the difference. Top it off with a fried egg and some Pan-Fried Sweet Plantains (page 139), and it is even more of a winner.

Makes: 4 servings
Cook Time: 20 minutes

Salmon

2 lb (907 g) skinless salmon fillets, cut into 2-inch (5-cm) cubes
¼ cup (60 ml) lemon juice (about 1 lemon)
1 tsp garlic powder
1 tbsp (7 g) onion powder
1 tbsp (2 g) parsley flakes
½ tsp salt plus a pinch, divided
1 tsp cayenne pepper, divided
¼ cup (55 g) ghee
3 tomatoes, diced
4 cloves (16 g) garlic, grated
1 tbsp (15 ml) coconut aminos
1 tsp dried oregano
½ cup (120 ml) vegetable broth
¼ cup (15 g) Italian parsley, finely chopped

Creamy Farine Polenta

2 cups (480 ml) vegetable broth
1 cup (170 g) farine
½ tsp salt
1 tbsp (5 g) nutritional yeast
1 cup (240 ml) full-fat coconut milk
¼ cup (58 g) almond cream cheese

To make the salmon, add the salmon cubes to a bowl and drizzle with lemon juice. Combine the garlic powder, onion powder, parsley flakes, ½ teaspoon of salt and ½ teaspoon of cayenne pepper. Add the seasoning mixture to the salmon and mix well. Set aside and let marinate at room temperature for 15 minutes.

Heat a skillet over medium heat. Add the ghee. When the ghee is hot, but not burning, add the salmon in a single layer. Cook on one side until brown, about 1 minute, then flip. Continue to cook and flip until all the sides are brown, then remove from the pan and set aside.

Add the tomatoes and a pinch of salt to the skillet. Continue to cook, stirring often, until the tomatoes are mushy. Add the garlic, coconut aminos, ½ teaspoon of cayenne pepper and oregano. Mix and continue to cook over medium heat for 1 minute, then add ½ cup (120 ml) of vegetable broth, cover and reduce the heat to low. Simmer until the liquid reduces by half and the sauce thickens. Mix in the parsley.

To make the farine polenta, bring the vegetable broth up to a boil in a saucepan over medium heat, then add the farine, salt and nutritional yeast and mix to combine. Let cook for about 2 minutes, then remove from the heat. Add the coconut milk and almond cream cheese and stir until fully combined. Cover and let the farine reconstitute before serving, about 5 minutes. The farine should look like corn polenta in texture and be a bit loose but not runny. If the farine becomes too thick before you are ready to serve, add a bit more coconut milk to loosen.

To serve, add the polenta to a bowl, top with a few pieces of salmon, then drizzle (or drench depending on your preference) with the sauce.

PLANTAIN AND BACON FRITTERS

Plantain fritters are typically made with crushed sweet plantains incorporated into a batter and fried. My version is a savory fritter made with shredded yellow plantains and bacon (feel free to use Paleo-friendly turkey bacon). I use eggs and cassava flour to bind the plantain and bacon together and keep this recipe Paleo. It is perfect for meal prep or a grab-and-go breakfast. Once you see how easy they are to whip up, you'll be making them often. Turn up the flavor and serve them with some Wiri Wiri Ranch Dressing (page 155).

Makes: 12 fritters
Cook Time: 12 minutes

¼ cup (55 g) coconut oil or similar, divided

1 small yellow onion, diced

1 tsp salt, plus a pinch, divided

4 cloves (16 g) garlic, grated

2 large yellow plantains (firm with no black spots), peeled (page 159)

¼ cup (15 g) Italian parsley, finely chopped

6 strips of crunchy Paleo-friendly bacon, crumbled

½ tsp smoked paprika

1 egg, beaten

¼ cup (60 g) cassava flour

1 wiri wiri pepper (optional), finely chopped

To Serve

Wiri Wiri Ranch Dressing (page 155)

In a skillet over medium heat, heat 1 tablespoon (14 g) of coconut oil. Add the diced onion and a pinch of salt. Cook about 3 minutes, or until the onion becomes a bit translucent. Add the garlic and continue to cook for 1 minute before removing from the heat.

Shred the plantains using the shredding side of a cheese grater. You can also easily do this in a food processor with a shredding blade.

In a large bowl, combine the shredded plantains, cooked onion and garlic, parsley, bacon, smoked paprika, remaining salt, egg, cassava flour and wiri wiri pepper and mix well.

In a skillet over medium heat, heat 3 tablespoons (41 g) of coconut oil. When the oil is hot, working in batches, add ¼ cup (60 ml) of the mixture at a time to the skillet. Press down the mixture with the back of a spoon and spread it out so that you make a thin disk. Cook until brown on the first side, about 1½ minutes. Then flip and continue to cook until brown on the other side, about 1 minute. Remove from the heat and drain on a plate lined with parchment paper. Repeat as needed until you've cooked all the fritters. Serve your fritters with a dollop of Wiri Wiri Ranch Dressing (page 155).

OVEN-ROASTED BAIGAN AND SHRIMP CHOKA

Baigan choka is a dish made by roasting eggplants, then adding spices and aromatics. Growing up, my mom always roasted baigan (eggplant) over an open flame to make choka. The smell of roasting choka filled the air. It is warm, smoky and comforting. These days I make a version of baigan choka in the oven and I add some shrimp. Serve this dish up with a side of Paleo-friendly Potato Roti (page 105) and enjoy.

Makes: 4 servings
Cook Time: 50 minutes

Eggplants

4 medium eggplants, cut in half lengthwise
1 large tomato
2 tbsp (30 ml) extra virgin olive oil, divided
1 head of garlic, cut in half
2 wiri wiri peppers, finely chopped
1 tsp salt

Shrimp

1 lb (454 g) small shrimp, peeled and deveined
½ tsp garlic powder
½ tsp onion powder
¼ tsp smoked paprika
½ tsp kosher salt
1 tbsp (15 ml) avocado oil or similar
5 scallions

To Serve

Potato Roti (page 105)

Preheat the oven to 400°F (205°C). Prepare a greased sheet pan.

To make the eggplants, place the eggplants cut side down on the prepared pan. Place the tomato on the sheet pan and drizzle with 1 tablespoon (15 ml) of extra virgin olive oil. Place the garlic in a sheet of aluminum foil. Drizzle with 1 tablespoon (15 ml) of oil and seal the foil wrap around the garlic, then add to the sheet pan. Roast for 40 to 45 minutes, or until the eggplant is tender and a bit mushy.

While the eggplant and tomato are roasting, prepare the shrimp. In a bowl, combine the shrimp, garlic powder, onion powder, smoked paprika and kosher salt and let sit for 10 to 15 minutes. Heat a skillet over high heat. Add the avocado oil and when it is hot, but not smoking, add the seasoned shrimp. Cook for about 1 minute on each side but be careful not to overcook the shrimp. Add the scallions and cook for 30 seconds. Remove from the heat and set aside.

When the eggplant is ready, remove the flesh from the skin and add to a bowl. Roughly chop the tomatoes before adding to the eggplant. Remove the garlic cloves from the foil and skins, then add to the bowl with the eggplant and tomatoes. Add the finely chopped wiri wiri peppers, scallions and salt and mix until fully combined, crushing the garlic cloves with the back of the spoon. For a smooth baigan choka you can add the mixture to a food processor for a few pulses or pulse with an immersion blender before adding the shrimp. Add the cooked shrimp and serve this up with some delicious Potato Roti (page 105).

PLANTAIN QUICHE

Everyone loves a good quiche. This is my Paleo-friendly quiche recipe with a bit of Caribbean flare. It is no secret that I love plantains. I get excited whenever I can use them in a recipe. So naturally I was thrilled to use them as a crust in this quiche. This recipe is great for meal prep. It makes a large quiche that can easily be reheated and enjoyed on its own or paired with some bacon or sausage.

Makes: 1 (10-inch [25-cm]) quiche
Cook Time: 50 minutes

3 yellow plantains (with few black spots), peeled (page 159) and cut into 2-inch (5-cm) rounds
4 cups (960 ml) water (or enough water to cover the plantains)
1 tsp sea salt, divided
½ small red bell pepper, diced
4 scallions, finely chopped
8 large eggs
½ cup (125 g) almond ricotta
½ cup (120 ml) coconut cream
1 tsp garlic powder
1 tsp onion powder
Pinch of black pepper
¼ tsp paprika

Grease a 10-inch (25-cm) quiche dish.

Into a saucepan over high heat, add the plantains, water and ½ teaspoon of sea salt. Cover and cook until the plantains are fork tender, about 10 minutes. Drain and crush the plantains with a fork and spread evenly into the bottom of the quiche dish. Then add the red bell peppers and scallions and set aside.

Preheat the oven to 350°F (175°C). In a large mixing bowl, combine the eggs, almond ricotta, coconut cream, garlic powder, onion powder, ½ teaspoon of salt, black pepper and paprika and mix until the coconut cream and almond ricotta are well combined. You could also do this in a blender and blend for 1 minute. Pour the mixture over the crushed plantains, red bell peppers and scallions.

Bake for 40 to 45 minutes, or until the center of the quiche is set and still a little jiggly. It will continue to cook as it cools. Allow to cool for 10 minutes, then slice up and serve.

POTATO ROTI

My mother is a master roti-making machine. She made roti almost every day during my childhood. Her flaky parathas are heavenly. She made potato rotis less often than parathas but they were still divine. She almost always made potato roti when she made Red Stew Chicken (page 36). I remember dipping pieces of roti into the stew and mixing the potato filling with the gravy. It was delicious. This is my gluten-free, grain-free, Paleo-friendly version of my mother's potato roti recipe. I use white potatoes in this recipe, but if white potatoes are not part of your Paleo diet you can use cassava or sweet potatoes.

Makes: 4 servings
Cook Time: 20 minutes

Dough

2 tbsp (8 g) psyllium husk
¾ cup (180 ml) hot water
1 cup (240 g) cassava flour
1 tsp baking powder
Pinch of salt

Filling

1 lb (454 g) white potatoes, peeled and diced
4 cups (960 ml) water (or enough water to cover the potatoes)
¾ tsp salt, divided
3 scallions, thinly sliced
2 wiri wiri peppers, habanero or other chili pepper, seeds and veins removed, finely chopped
1 tsp onion powder
1 tsp garlic powder
½ tsp Geera (page 157)
¼ cup (55 g) ghee (optional)

To Serve

Red Stew Chicken (page 36)

To make the dough, combine the psyillum husk and hot water in a cup and let sit for 5 minutes. A gel will form. In a bowl, combine cassava flour, baking powder and salt. Mix well. Add the psyllium gel and mix into the cassava flour mixture until it forms a smooth dough ball. Cover and let rest for 30 minutes.

To make the filling, while the dough is resting, add the potatoes to a medium-sized saucepan. Cover the potatoes with the water. Add ½ teaspoon of salt to the water. Bring to a boil, uncovered, over high heat. Continue to cook until the potatoes can easily be crushed with a fork, about 10 minutes. Drain the potatoes in a colander, rinse with cold water and set aside.

Crush the potatoes until smooth. If you have a potato ricer, that works well here. Otherwise, a potato masher or a fork will do. Add the scallions, wiri wiri peppers, onion powder, garlic powder, Geera and ¼ teaspoon of salt to the crushed potatoes. Mix well and set aside.

Divide the dough ball into eight pieces. Shape each piece into a ball, then place each ball between parchment paper and roll with a rolling pin into a thin, flat disk. Add ¼ cup (60 ml) of the potato filling to the dough and spread evenly, leaving about ½ inch (1.3 cm) of space along the edges. Place another flat disk on top of the potato-covered dough and pinch the edges to seal.

This step is optional but if you would like to have neat edges, you may place a circular bowl over the roti and use a knife to cut around the shape of the bowl.

Repeat to make all four potato rotis.

Heat a cast iron skillet over medium heat. One at a time, add a potato roti to the skillet. Cook for about 3 minutes, then flip to the other side. Continue to cook for another 3 minutes, or until brown spots appear. You should see air pockets forming on the roti and the roti may completely inflate, although this is not necessary. Remove from the heat and wrap in a kitchen towel to keep warm. Repeat until all the rotis are cooked. When the rotis cool, brush the tops with ghee (if using). Serve your roti with some Red Stew Chicken (page 36).

EGG AND CAULI-FLOWER RICE

Eggs and rice are comfort in a bowl for me. As a Caribbean person, I always had cooked rice in my refrigerator and would whip up some fried eggs and rice whenever I needed a quick meal. I often made this on busy days when I forgot to have breakfast but needed to make a quick lunch. Now, as a Caribbean Paleo person, I always have frozen cauliflower rice in my freezer, typically my Toasted Cauliflower Rice (page 136)! So now, I make Egg and Cauliflower Rice. This recipe is quick and easy to pull together when you need a one-pot or one-bowl kind of meal. This recipe serves one or two, depending on your appetite!

Makes: 2 servings
Cook Time: 20 minutes

3 tbsp (45 ml) olive oil or similar, divided

10 oz (274 g) frozen riced cauliflower, completely defrosted

½ tsp coarse salt

1 tomato, diced

4 cloves (16 g) garlic, grated

2 eggs, beaten

Freshly cracked black pepper

3 scallions, diced

To Serve

Pickled Cucumbers (page 144)

Mango and Wiri Wiri Pepper Sauce (page 147)

Heat a skillet on high heat until it is almost to the point of smoking (page 51). Add 1 tablespoon (15 ml) of oil and the riced cauliflower in an even layer. Cook for 2 to 3 minutes without stirring, or until the rice starts to brown. Sprinkle with the coarse salt and stir to combine. Continue to cook for 1 to 2 minutes, or until most of the rice is brown and toasted. Transfer the rice to a bowl.

Return the skillet to medium heat, then add 2 tablespoons (30 ml) of olive oil. Add the tomato and garlic and cook until the tomatoes start to soften. Add the beaten eggs and the cracked black pepper and stir. Cook until the eggs look like scrambled eggs, then add the cauliflower rice back to the skillet. Add the scallions and continue to cook for 1 to 2 minutes, stirring until the rice and eggs are combined. Serve hot with a bit of Pickled Cucumbers (page 144) and Mango and Wiri Wiri Pepper Sauce (page 147).

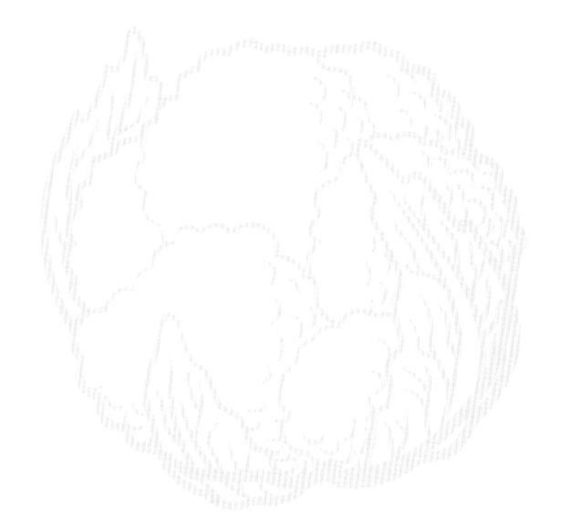

CODFISH BULJOL

Buljol is a Trinidadian term for a sort of fish salad. Typically, this dish is made with salted fish. However, in Guyana we make fish chokas with roasted fish and fresh aromatics and it is very similar to a buljol. I created this recipe as a mash-up between the two dishes: oven-baked cod, flaked then seasoned with raw onions, peppers and tomatoes. Serve this up for breakfast with a side of Paleo-friendly crackers or over some Pan-Fried Sweet Plantains (page 139).

Makes: 4 servings
Cook Time: 10 minutes

1 lb (454 g) skinless cod fillets
¼ cup (60 ml) lemon juice (about 1 lemon)
3 tbsp (45 ml) avocado oil, divided
2 tsp (10 g) onion powder
1 tsp garlic powder
1½ tsp (10 g) coarse salt, divided
3 firm tomatoes, diced, seeds removed
1 cup (110 g) diced red onion
3 cloves (16 g) garlic, grated
¼ cup (4 g) culantro leaves or cilantro, finely chopped
3 wiri wiri chilies or jalapeños, finely chopped (optional)
1 tbsp (15 ml) lime juice (about 1 lime)

To Serve

Paleo-friendly crackers
Pan-Fried Sweet Plantains (page 139)

Preheat the oven to 400°F (205°C). Prepare a greased baking sheet.

Pat the codfish dry before seasoning. Drizzle the lemon juice over the fish, then drizzle with 2 tablespoons (30 ml) of avocado oil. Add the onion powder, garlic powder and 1 teaspoon of coarse salt, making sure that both sides of the fillets are fully coated. Place the fish on the prepared sheet and bake for 10 to 12 minutes, or until the flesh becomes opaque and flakes easily with a fork. Remove from the oven and let rest for 5 minutes.

Add the fish to a bowl and flake with a fork. Add the tomatoes, red onion, garlic, culantro, wiri wiri chilies (if using), lime juice, the remaining avocado oil and remaining salt. The chilies make it a really spicy dish, so feel free to use fewer or skip them all together. Mix well. Taste and add a pinch of salt if needed. Serve with a side of Paleo-friendly crackers or some Pan-Fried Sweet Plantains (page 139).

FARINE PORRIDGE

Were you an oatmeal-in-the-morning kind of person before going Paleo? Me too. I was also a cornmeal-porridge kind of person. I missed having these simple warm breakfast options until I started using farine to make porridge. This is not a new thing for Caribbean people, but it was something I had completely forgotten about. Farine is a cassava meal made mostly by Indigenous Caribbean people. It is used widely throughout the Caribbean for many dishes including a version of this porridge. If you miss having a warm, hearty breakfast that's simple and easy to put together, give this recipe a try.

Makes: 4 servings
Cook Time: 15 minutes

4 cups (960 ml) almond milk
2 cardamom pods
1 tbsp (5 g) whole cloves
2 cinnamon sticks
1 cup (170 g) farine
1 cup (240 ml) coconut milk
1 tsp grated nutmeg

To Serve

Paleo-friendly sweetener of your choice
1 cup (145 g) raisins
1 mango, diced
Coconut flakes
¼ cup (60 g) almond butter

Into a saucepan over medium heat, add the almond milk, cardamom pods, cloves and cinnamon sticks and bring to a boil. Add the farine and mix well. Reduce the heat to low and continue to cook until the farine becomes completely reconstituted, about 5 minutes. Add the coconut milk and nutmeg and mix well, then remove from the heat.

To serve, add your sweetener of choice and top each serving with raisins, diced mango, coconut flakes and a drizzle of almond butter.

A LIL' SOMETHING SWEET

I didn't grow up having dessert to finish off a meal. Desserts were reserved for special occasions and holidays. Even then we ate the dessert independent of meals. For instance, you might have a slice of cake in the afternoon before you had dinner, but never after dinner. That changed so much after moving to the U.S. Dessert became a big part of meals and I craved something sweet after meals.

Now that I'm Paleo, I'm back to looking at desserts as just a little something sweet if you want it, but not as part of a meal. I'm happy to be back where I started as this has really helped with sugar cravings. This chapter is dedicated to those moments when you want a lil' something sweet. My favorite recipe in this chapter is the Soursop Ice Cream (page 115). It is so simple to make with just a few ingredients, and it is so delicious. It's also really tasty when blended into a soursop milkshake and topped off with extra nutmeg. Sugar Roti (page 123) also has a special place in my heart as it immediately reminds me of my late grandmother, Evelyn. If you want a place to start in this chapter, start with these two recipes.

SOURSOP ICE CREAM

When I was little, we lived about a 10-minute walk from Demico (a popular food chain in Guyana). They sold the most delicious soursop ice cream. On Sunday afternoons, my parents, my brothers and I walked down to Demico, bought our ice cream cones and walked back home savoring every lick. This is my coconut-based version of that ice cream. It is dairy-free, refined sugar–free, fuss-free and oh so yummy.

Makes: 3 pints (1.4 L)
Freeze Time: 5 hours

2 (13.5-oz [400-ml]) cans coconut cream

½ cup (120 ml) full-fat coconut milk

½ cup (120 ml) maple syrup

1 tsp vanilla extract

½ tsp grated nutmeg

Pinch of salt

14 oz (396 g) soursop pulp, frozen

Into a blender, scoop out all the solidified coconut cream and none of the liquid that settles at the bottom of the can. Add the coconut milk, maple syrup, vanilla extract, grated nutmeg, pinch of salt and the frozen soursop pulp. Blend on low until the mixture is smooth and creamy, under a minute.

Pour the mixture in a freezer-safe container. Cover and freeze for at least 5 hours, or until set.

NOTES: You can find soursop pulp in the freezer section of most Mexican markets. You may also find fresh soursop (when it is in season) at Asian markets. If using fresh soursop, remove the seeds from the pulp before freezing.

If the ice cream is frozen for more than 5 hours, let it sit at room temperature for 15 minutes before serving or it will be hard to scoop.

PLANTAIN CINNAMON ROLLS

It is no secret that Caribbean folks love plantains (raises hand), especially sweet, ripe plantains. Therefore, plantains as a quick and easy dessert is a no-brainer. This is not a traditional Caribbean dish, but a fusion of sorts. For this dish you want to choose plantains that have more black spots than yellow. The plantains will be sweet enough to skip added sugar, but if you want to add a little bit of maple syrup or coconut sugar to the cinnamon butter, go for it!

Makes: 4 (4-oz [120-ml]) servings

Cook Time: 10–15 minutes

¼ cup (60 g) ghee or grass-fed butter, divided, plus extra for greasing ramekins

1 tbsp (10 g) cinnamon

3 ripe plantains (black with a few yellow spots), peeled (page 159)

To Serve

Soursop Ice Cream (page 115)

Preheat the oven to 450°F (230°C). Prepare four 4-ounce (120-ml) greased, round, individual ramekins.

Combine the ghee and the cinnamon to form a spread and set aside. Slice each plantain lengthwise into four slices. Then spread about 1 teaspoon of the ghee and cinnamon mixture on one side of each of the plantain slices.

Starting from the wall of the ramekin and working in, add a buttered plantain slice to a ramekin so that it resembles a cinnamon bun or roll. Repeat with the other plantain slices. Then top each of these plantain rolls with a teaspoon of the butter and cinnamon mixture.

Bake for 15 minutes, or until the tops of the rolls are golden brown, then remove from the oven and them let cool before serving. Top with a scoop of Soursop Ice Cream (page 115)!

NOTE: To make these using an air fryer, air fry the plantain rolls at 450°F (230°C) for 10 minutes.

COCONUT SWEET BREAD

Coconut breads or cakes are popular throughout the Caribbean. They are typically packed with freshly grated coconut and mixed dry fruits. Think banana bread with walnuts and raisins, but instead of bananas, the star is coconut. This bread is great as a coffee cake or with a cup of tea (my preference). You can use any combination of Paleo-friendly fruit and nuts you like.

Makes: 1 (9 x 5-inch [23 x 13-cm]) loaf
Cook Time: 40–45 minutes

¼ cup (60 ml) melted coconut oil
¼ cup (60 ml) coconut milk
5 eggs
¼ cup (60 g) coconut sugar
¾ cup (180 g) cassava flour
¾ cup (72 g) superfine almond flour
¼ tsp salt
1 tbsp (14 g) baking powder
3 cups (280 g) grated coconut (fresh or frozen)
½ cup (73 g) raisins
¼ cup (40 g) dried cherries
½ cup (40 g) dried currants
½ cup (60 g) walnuts

Preheat the oven to 350°F (175°C). Prepare a greased loaf pan lined with parchment paper.

In a mixing bowl, combine the coconut oil, milk, eggs and coconut sugar. Whisk until the coconut sugar dissolves, about 3 minutes. Add the cassava flour, almond flour, salt and baking powder and whisk until fully combined. Then, using a wooden spoon or rubber spatula, mix in the grated coconut, raisins, cherries and currants.

Pour the batter into the prepared loaf pan. Top with the walnuts. Bake for 40 to 45 minutes, or until golden brown and a toothpick inserted into the bread comes out clean. Remove from the oven and allow to cool for 20 minutes before slicing and serving or it may be crumbly.

COCONUT BAKED CUSTARD

Baked custard is one of those desserts that you don't really think of as dessert. However, in Guyana it is a well-known dessert. My husband loves a good baked custard and I would make the traditional recipe for him all the time. When I became Paleo, I could no longer enjoy all that dairy and sugar, so I remixed the recipe. This is my coconut milk–based, Paleo-friendly baked custard and it is so yummy. The recipe requires making your own Paleo evaporated coconut milk, so allow extra time to get this part done, but after that the remaining steps come together quickly.

Makes: 6 servings
Cook Time: 40 minutes

3 (13.5-oz [400-ml]) cans full-fat coconut milk
¼ cup (60 ml) maple syrup
4 large eggs
1 tsp vanilla extract
1 tsp grated nutmeg
3 cups (720 ml) hot water

Preheat the oven to 350°F (175°C). Prepare a greased baking dish or individual ramekins. Prepare a deep baking tray.

In a medium-sized saucepan over high heat, add the coconut milk and maple syrup. Bring to a boil. Boil for about 2 minutes, continuously stirring. The mixture will get frothy, so keep an eye out that it doesn't overflow. As soon as it gets foamy and starts to rise, reduce the heat to medium-low and simmer for 40 minutes, gently stirring every 10 minutes to avoid burning. The mixture should reduce by about 25 percent.

Whisk together the eggs, vanilla extract and nutmeg. Temper the eggs by whisking 1 tablespoon (15 ml) of hot evaporated coconut milk at a time into the eggs. Continue until you've added about ½ cup (120 ml) of the evaporated coconut milk, then add the remaining milk all at once to the eggs and whisk.

Pour the mixture into the prepared baking dish or ramekins. Then place the baking dish or ramekins in a deep baking tray on the center rack of the oven. Pour the hot water into the baking tray until it comes halfway up the side of the baking dish or ramekins. Bake for 40 minutes, or until the custard sets. It may still feel a little jiggly but should not be too loose. Serve warm or chill in the refrigerator and serve cold.

SUGAR ROTI

My grandmother Evelyn made sugar roti whenever we visited her home. She stuffed brown sugar into roti dough and made the most delicious sweet treat. Sometimes she rubbed butter on the roti and served it up hot. Sticky melted sugar oozed from the roti as we ripped pieces off, blowing vigorously while shoving it into our mouths. Even now as I write this I can see my cousins and myself chewing and huffing air into our mouths to cool down the hot sugar. I created this Paleo Sugar Roti in honor of her and this memory. This recipe is grain-free, refined sugar-free and completely Paleo, and can be enjoyed with a dab of ghee.

Makes: 4 sugar rotis
Cook Time: 20 minutes

2 tbsp (8 g) psyllium husk
¾ cup (180 ml) boiling hot water
1 cup (240 g) cassava flour
1 tsp baking powder
Pinch of salt
¼ cup (60 g) coconut sugar

Combine the psyllium husk and hot water in a cup and let sit for 5 minutes. A gel will form. In a bowl, combine cassava flour, baking powder and salt. Mix well. Add the psyllium gel in the cassava flour mixture and mix until it forms a smooth dough ball. Cover and let rest for 30 minutes.

Divide the dough ball into eight pieces. Shape each piece into a ball, then place each ball between parchment paper and roll with a rolling pin into a thin, flat disk. Cover one disk with 1 tablespoon (14 g) of coconut sugar, leaving about ½ inch (1.3 cm) along the edge sugar free. Place another flat disk on top of the sugar-covered dough and pinch the edges to seal. Repeat to make all four sugar rotis.

This step is optional but if you would like to have neat edges, you may place a circular bowl over the roti and use a knife to cut around the shape of the bowl.

Heat a cast iron skillet over medium heat. Add one sugar roti to the skillet and cook for about 3 minutes, then flip to the other side. Continue to cook for another 3 minutes, or until brown spots appear. You should see air pockets forming on the roti and it may completely inflate. Do not overcook, or the sugar will caramelize and taste bitter. Remove from the heat and wrap in a kitchen towel to keep warm. Repeat until all the rotis are cooked.

CASHEW AND ALMOND PUNCH

Peanut punch is a traditional Caribbean beverage made with raw peanuts soaked and blended with milk, although many people make it with peanut butter. This is my Paleo version of that popular Caribbean treat. I use cashews and almond milk instead and it is delicious: raw cashews, dry roasted, then blended with almond milk, almond butter and warm spices. The cashews give this drink a similar texture to peanut punch. Try it sweetened with a little bit of maple syrup or coconut sugar and you will be in heaven.

Makes: 4 servings
Cook Time: 12–17 minutes

2 cups (300 g) raw cashews
2 cups (480 ml) unsweetened almond milk
¼ cup (60 g) unsweetened almond butter
1 tsp vanilla extract
1 tsp grated nutmeg
½ tsp ground cinnamon
¼ cup (60 ml) maple syrup or coconut sugar

Preheat the oven to 350°F (175°C). Place the cashews in a single layer on a parchment paper–lined sheet pan. Roast for 10 to 15 minutes, or until the cashews are light brown. Remove from the oven and allow to cool. Then add to a blender with the almond milk, almond butter, vanilla extract, grated nutmeg, ground cinnamon and maple syrup.

Blend until completely smooth, about 2 minutes, then pour over ice and enjoy.

SORREL ICED TEA

Sorrel or hibiscus tea (also called Flor de Jamaica and Zobo) is one of my favorite drinks. This refreshing sorrel iced tea is perfect for hot summer days or the heat of the tropics: sorrel blossoms, warm spices and black tea, brewed and steeped for a tasty iced beverage. Traditionally, sorrel is not combined with tea, but I love iced teas and thought this would be a tasty remix and it did not disappoint.

Makes: 4 servings
Cook Time: 20 minutes

4 cups (960 ml) water
1 cinnamon stick
1 tsp whole cloves
2-inch (5-cm) piece of dried orange peel
2 black tea bags
½ cup (20 g) dried sorrel blossoms
1 cup (240 ml) maple syrup or sweetener of choice
1 navel orange, sliced

In a medium saucepan over high heat, add the water, cinnamon stick, whole cloves, orange peel and tea bags. Bring to a boil. Add the dried sorrel blossoms to the pot and reduce the heat to low. Cover and simmer for 20 minutes. Remove from the heat and sweeten with maple syrup. Allow to cool completely. Strain using a fine-mesh strainer lined with muslin cloth. Garnish with orange slices and serve over ice.

THE BASICS

There are a few recipes that every Caribbean home cook should have handy. Some are seasoning blends and sauces that are added to many dishes. They are good to make ahead and store in the refrigerator. Others are pickles and condiments that are added to meals.

Blended seasoning is a key part of protein prep in Guyanese and other Caribbean kitchens. Fresh herbs and spices blended into a paste are often used as the first step of meat prep, after washing the meat of course. I know that meat washing is very controversial, but it is a food preparation step that Caribbean people still practice.

Pickles, hot sauce and condiments are a must for Caribbean meals. I don't make most of my recipes spicy because I am cooking for my family, which includes three young children. However, I always add pepper sauce or some spicy condiment to my plate and my husband's plate before serving each meal.

GREEN SEASONING

Green seasoning is a Caribbean pantry must-have. It is similar to what pesto is to Italians and sofrito is to the Latinx community. It is the base for this trio of seasonings. Growing up, every Sunday, my mom made a batch of green seasoning immediately after she came home from the market. She then seasoned all her meats, parceled them off according to how she planned to cook them over the coming week, and stored them in the freezer. I've modified this tradition slightly in my own cooking. I make a fresh batch of green seasoning when I am prepping a dish that needs it and I freeze the excess in ice cube trays to use in dishes that need a little flavor boost.

Makes: 1½ cups (360 ml) per variation

Prep Time: 10 minutes

Basic Green Seasoning

1 large yellow onion, roughly chopped

4 scallions

1 head garlic, peeled

1 bunch culantro or cilantro

½ cup (30 g) Italian parsley

1 bunch thyme leaves, removed from the stems

Spicy Green Seasoning

1 batch Basic Green Seasoning ingredients

2-inch (5-cm) piece ginger

1 large chili pepper (like Scotch bonnet or habanero) or 3 wiri wiri chilies

Green Seasoning for Rice Dishes

1 batch Basic Green Seasoning ingredients

1 cup (24 g) Guyanese Marrid Man Poke (may use Thai basil)

1 medium tomato

To make Basic Green Seasoning, combine the yellow onion, scallions, garlic, culantro, parsley and thyme leaves in a food processor and process until you are left with a smooth paste. This should take about 1 minute. Transfer your Basic Green Seasoning in an airtight container (such as a Mason jar) and store in the refrigerator for up to 1 week. You may also transfer the seasoning to an ice cube mold and freeze into ready-to-use, flavor-packed seasoning cubes.

To make Spicy Green Seasoning, combine Basic Green Seasoning ingredients, ginger and chili pepper in a food processor and process until you are left with a smooth paste. This should take about 1 minute. Transfer your Spicy Green Seasoning in an airtight container (such as a Mason jar) and store in the refrigerator for up to 1 week. You may also transfer the seasoning to an ice cube mold and freeze into ready-to-use, flavor-packed seasoning cubes.

To make Green Seasoning for Rice Dishes, combine Basic Green Seasoning ingredients, Guyanese Marrid Man Poke and tomato in a food processor and process until you are left with a smooth paste. This should take about 1 minute. Transfer your Green Seasoning for Rice Dishes in an airtight container (such as a Mason jar) and store in the refrigerator for up to 1 week. You may also transfer the seasoning to an ice cube mold and freeze into ready-to-use, flavor-packed seasoning cubes.

JERK SEASONING

Jerk is uniquely Jamaican. It is a method of cooking, as well as a spice rub and a marinade. It is said that the word jerk is linked to the Spanish word charqui, *which refers to smoked, dried meat. This makes a lot of sense, as authentic jerk chicken is smoked over pimento wood and leaves. Today, the world knows jerk mostly as a very distinct flavor that is predominantly linked to allspice or pimento berries. This Jerk Seasoning is exploding with that deep, rich jerk flavor. Traditional Jerk seasoning is not Paleo-compatible as it often has added sugar or browning, a dark caramel made with cane sugar. I use coconut aminos in this recipe as a browning and sugar substitute, therefore making this recipe Paleo. Make a double batch of this and stick it in the refrigerator, because trust me, you will want to marinate all your meats with this!*

Makes: 2 cups
Prep Time: 10 minutes

½ yellow onion, peeled and roughly chopped
3 scallions
5 sprigs thyme, leaves removed from the stems
2 wiri wiri peppers, 1 Scotch bonnet pepper or 1 habanero pepper
2-inch (5-cm) piece ginger, peeled and chopped
8 cloves (32 g) garlic
1 tbsp (11 g) allspice, whole or ground
½ tbsp (5 g) ground cinnamon
1 tsp nutmeg, ground or freshly grated
½ tsp kosher salt
¼ tsp black pepper
½ tsp yellow mustard
¼ cup (60 ml) coconut aminos
1 tbsp (15 ml) white vinegar, apple cider vinegar or red wine vinegar
1 tbsp (15 ml) avocado oil or similar

Into a food processor bowl, add the onion, scallions, thyme, wiri wiri peppers, ginger, garlic, allspice, cinnamon, nutmeg, kosher salt and black pepper and process until smooth. Add the mustard, then drizzle in the coconut aminos, vinegar and avocado oil and process until fully combined. Transfer the jerk seasoning to an airtight container, such as a Mason jar, and store in the refrigerator for up to a month.

NOTE: Following this recipe as written is very spicy. You may adjust the heat level by using half the amount of peppers listed or by removing the seeds and the veins from the peppers.

TAMARIND CHUTNEY

Tamarind chutney (called tamarind sour in Guyana) is a popular condiment added to most street food dishes. The tartness of the tamarind when paired with spices and a hint of sweetness adds a light and refreshing contrast to most of the fried foods served by street vendors.

Servings: 1 cup
Cook Time: 20 minutes

¼ cup (60 g) tamarind paste
1 cup (135 g) pitted dates
3 scallions
2 cloves (8 g) garlic
3 wiri wiri peppers, ½ habanero or Scotch bonnet pepper
1 cup (240 ml) water
½ tsp salt
1 tsp Geera (page 157)

In a blender, combine the tamarind paste, dates, scallions, garlic, wiri wiri peppers, water, salt and Geera and blend until smooth. Add to a saucepan over medium heat and bring to a boil. Boil until the mixture thickens, about 5 minutes. Remove from the heat and allow to cool completely before serving. Store in the refrigerator for up to 2 weeks.

NOTE: Following this recipe as written is very spicy. You may adjust the heat level by using half the amount of peppers listed or by removing the seeds and the veins from the peppers.

TOASTED CAULIFLOWER RICE

Rice is such a Caribbean staple that when I first started limiting rice in my diet, I refused to accept cauliflower rice as a substitute. I protested that this is not rice! Over time I learned to cook the riced cauliflower so that it tasted as close to the real-deal rice as possible. I prefer frozen riced cauliflower over fresh because it has more riced stalk than florets and this makes the texture more akin to regular rice. Trust me on this one! I am a girl who ate rice almost every day of her life. I often make this recipe in batches and then freeze it for an easy weeknight side for stews.

Makes: 4 servings
Cook Time: 10 minutes

20 oz (547 g) frozen riced cauliflower, completely defrosted

2 tbsp (28 g) coconut oil or ghee

Salt to taste

Heat a large skillet over medium heat. Test the skillet for readiness by sprinkling a few drops of water on the skillet. If the water sizzles and evaporates, it is not ready. If the water droplet dances on the surface of the skillet, it is ready.

Add your defrosted riced cauliflower to the skillet and let it sit untouched for 3 to 5 minutes, or until most of the moisture evaporates and it starts to brown a little. Toss and continue to cook until most of the riced pieces are brown.

Add coconut oil and salt and mix well. Remove from the heat and serve as a side of "rice" for your favorite dishes.

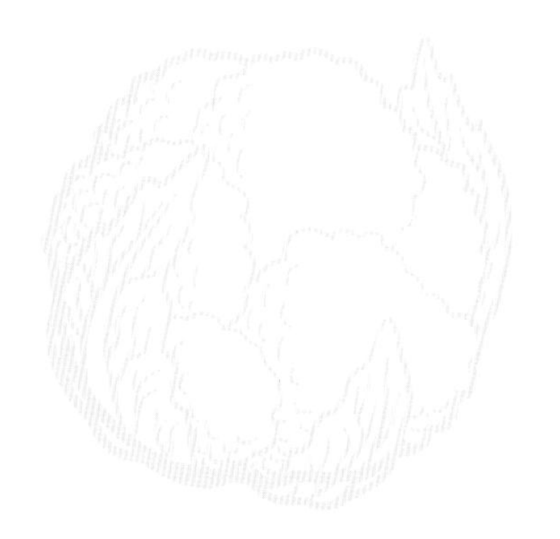

PAN-FRIED SWEET PLANTAINS

No Caribbean meal is complete without a side of pan-fried sweet plantains. This simple side offers a bit of sweetness to any dish and is naturally Paleo, so no adjustments needed. Choosing the right plantain is crucial. Look for plantains that are mostly black with a few yellow spots. Feel the plantain by pressing gently with your thumb. The plantains should be soft but not mushy.

Makes: 4 servings
Cook Time: 10 minutes

2 ripe plantains (mostly black), peeled (page 159)
¼ cup (55 g) coconut oil
Pinch of kosher salt

Prepare a plate lined with parchment paper.

Cut the plantains into thirds, then into three to four pieces. You should have pieces that are about 2 x ¼ inches (5 x ½ cm) in size.

In a frying pan on medium to medium-low heat, heat the coconut oil. When the oil is hot, add the plantain pieces in a single layer and cook until they're dark brown on the oil side, about 2 minutes. Flip and continue to cook until both sides are dark brown.

Remove the plantains from the heat and place on the prepared plate. Sprinkle with a pinch of kosher salt.

JERK SAUCE

I'm not exaggerating when I say that I put this jerk sauce on EVERYTHING! If you give this recipe a try you will be doing the same. The star of this sauce is undoubtedly allspice. Allspice is a single spice (not a spice blend) and it is what gives jerk seasoning its unique taste. It tastes a little like nutmeg, cinnamon, cloves and black pepper combined and it is so good. When I first went Paleo, there were no store-bought Paleo-compatible jerk sauces. Back then, store-bought jerk sauces all had added sugar. So I created my own Paleo jerk sauce and I have been using this at home ever since. Make a batch of this sauce and you'll find yourself dipping into it with everything you can find. It pairs perfectly well with my Jerk Chicken Under a Brick (page 16).

Servings: 1½ cups (360 ml)
Cook Time: 10 minutes

1 yellow onion, peeled and chopped
3 scallions, peeled and chopped
5 sprigs fresh thyme, leaves removed from the stems
1 Scotch bonnet or habanero pepper
2-inch (5-cm) piece ginger, peeled and chopped
8 cloves garlic
¼ cup (60 ml) avocado oil or similar
1 tbsp (5 g) allspice (pimento berries), whole or ground
½ tbsp ground cinnamon
1 tsp nutmeg, ground or freshly grated
1 tsp kosher salt
¼ tsp black pepper
¼ cup (60 ml) Paleo-friendly ketchup
½ tsp yellow mustard
¼ cup (60 ml) coconut aminos
1½ cup (360 ml) water

Add the onion, scallions, thyme, Scotch bonnet pepper and garlic to a food processor and blend until smooth, about 2 minutes. Then heat a pan on medium heat and add the avocado oil. When the oil is hot, add the pureed seasoning, then the allspice, cinnamon and nutmeg. Cook for about 2 minutes, stirring often, or until the seasoning starts to stick to the bottom of the pan. Then add the kosher salt, black pepper and ketchup. Mix together well and cook for another minute to allow the ketchup to caramelize, about 1 minute.

Add the mustard and coconut aminos and cook for another minute. Then add the water, and stir to dissolve any stuck-on ingredients from the bottom of the pan. Continue to cook on medium heat, then bring to a boil. Boil until the sauce reduces and gets to your desired thickness, 3 to 4 minutes, then remove from the heat and allow to cool. Store the cooled sauce in the refrigerator in an airtight container (like a Mason jar) for up to 2 weeks. You can use this sauce as a garnish for cooked meats or as a recipe starter for quick dishes.

NOTE: This sauce is very spicy. You may adjust the heat level by using half the amount of pepper listed or by removing the seeds and the veins from the pepper.

Jerk
Sauce

CURRY PASTE

Curry is one of my favorite things to cook. If you ask my children what their favorite meal is they will likely say chicken curry and roti. Most curries are naturally Paleo, but be sure to check your curry powder ingredients list to avoid fillers that are not Paleo-friendly. This recipe is my cheat for making a quick and easy curry dish no matter the protein. Make this curry paste ahead, store it in the refrigerator and just add protein whenever you need a quick curry dish.

Servings: 2 cups (480 ml)
Cook Time: 10 minutes

1 large yellow onion
2 scallions
¼ cup (4 g) cilantro
¼ cup (15 g) Italian parsley
8 cloves (32 g) garlic
2 wiri wiri peppers or ½ habanero pepper
1½ cups (360 ml) water, divided
¼ cup (25 g) Curry Powder (page 152)
¼ tsp ground turmeric
1 tsp ground coriander
2 tsp (2 g) Geera (page 157)
½ tsp Garam Masala (page 151)
¼ tsp paprika
1 tsp ground mustard
1 tsp kosher salt (optional)
¼ cup (60 ml) of avocado oil or similar
1–2 curry leaves (optional)
1 bay leaf

Add the onion, scallions, cilantro, parsley, garlic and wiri wiri peppers to a food processor. Process to form a smoothie-like consistency, and as you process, pour in ½ cup (120 ml) of water. If using a blender, add the water before blending.

Pour the blended seasoning in a bowl. Add the Curry Powder, ground turmeric, coriander, Geera, Garam Masala, paprika, ground mustard and kosher salt (if using) and mix together well.

Heat the avocado oil in a saucepan on high heat. When the oil is hot, add the curry leaves (if using). Be careful as the oil will splatter and can burn. Cook for a few seconds, then immediately add the seasoning mixture you prepared earlier, followed by the bay leaf.

Cook for about 5 minutes, stirring often, until the liquids cook down and the paste starts to brown, but be careful not to burn it. Add 1 cup (240 ml) of water. Stir to remove any stuck-on bits from the pan and bring to a boil. Reduce the heat to medium-low. Continue to cook for 1 to 2 minutes, constantly stirring, until the sauce thickens. Then remove from the heat and allow to cool completely. Add the curry paste to a Mason jar and store in the refrigerator for up to 2 weeks, or freeze in an ice cube tray.

NOTE: This recipe makes a spicy curry paste. You may adjust the heat level by using half the amount of peppers listed or by removing the seeds and the veins from the peppers. You may also skip the peppers all together.

PICKLED CUCUMBERS

I don't know how pickles became such a popular condiment for Guyanese meals (maybe the Chinese influence on our food), but I know that throughout my childhood they were on the side of almost every dish my mom served. My dad makes the best pickled cucumbers with salt, pepper, a pinch of sugar and a squeeze of lime juice. It is sweet, tangy, sour, crunchy and spicy all at the same time. He makes it just before he starts cooking and sticks it in the refrigerator. It is perfection. This is my Paleo version of that quick pickle and I promise you, you will want to add this to every meal, just like my dad does with his version.

Makes: 4–6 servings
Cook Time: 10 minutes

2 cups (480 ml) water
1 tbsp (11 g) allspice berries
1 tsp mustard seeds
2 tbsp (30 ml) coconut aminos
1 tsp coarse salt
2 wiri wiri peppers, roughly chopped
4 cloves (16 g) garlic, peeled and smashed
½ cup (120 ml) distilled white vinegar
2 Kirby (mini seedless) cucumbers, sliced

To make the pickle brine, add the water, allspice berries, mustard seeds and coconut aminos to a saucepan. Bring to a boil over high heat. Boil until the water reduces by half, about 5 minutes, then remove from the heat.

Add the coarse salt, wiri wiri peppers and garlic and stir to combine. Cover and let the mixture sit until it cools completely, about 10 minutes. Pour the mixture in a Mason jar or similar container. Add the vinegar and mix well. Add the sliced cucumbers, cover and let rest in the refrigerator for at least 30 minutes before serving. Use as a condiment.

NOTE: My dad makes his cucumbers a bit fancy before slicing them. He uses a fork to scrape lengthwise lines along the cucumber skin. Applying gentle pressure, glide the prongs of a fork in a downward motion along the cucumber skin. Rinse and pat dry. Then slice your cucumber into ¼-inch (6-mm)-thick slices.

MANGO AND WIRI WIRI PEPPER SAUCE

Wiri wiri pepper is a small cherry-like chili native to Guyana. Wiri wiri pepper sauce is the pride and joy of any Guyanese household. I want to say that the flavor is unlike any pepper sauce you've ever tasted because of my Guyanese pride, but you can also make this pepper sauce with habanero, Scotch bonnet or Trinidadian pimento pepper. Many households make their own special batch of this pepper sauce, adding in sour fruits and aromatics to suit their tastes. I'm adding some mangoes to mine and unlike when my dad makes it, I'm blending up my onion and garlic. My dad loves adding sliced onion and garlic to his pepper sauce, then picking the pieces out of the pepper sauce and eating them with his food, like a sort of pickled onions and garlic. This recipe is one of those recipes that are naturally Paleo and needed no adjustments for this book.

Makes: 3 cups (360 ml)
Prep Time: 10 minutes

1 large firm yellow mango, peeled, flesh cut away from the pit
2 cups (300 g) wiri wiri peppers, washed, stems removed
1 small yellow onion, peeled
6 cloves (24 g) garlic, peeled
1¼ cups (300 ml) white vinegar
1 tsp salt

Into a blender, add the mango flesh, wiri wiri peppers, onion, garlic, vinegar and salt. Blend until smooth, 1 to 2 minutes. Then pour the pepper sauce in a sterilized Mason jar. Cover and let rest on the kitchen counter at room temperature for about 2 weeks to allow the pepper sauce to ferment. You may also put the jar on a sunny windowsill to speed up the fermentation process. After 2 weeks, the pepper sauce is ready to be used. You may store your sauce in the refrigerator if you so choose but it is not necessary.

NOTE: Once fermented, there is no shelf life for pepper sauce. It will only go bad if it becomes contaminated. For this reason, it is important to use a clean utensil every time you take pepper sauce from the jar.

PASSION-FRUIT VINAI-GRETTE

Need a tasty Caribbean inspired Paleo salad dressing that is easy to make and has the brightness of tropical fruits? Then this recipe is a must-try. Passionfruit is one of my favorite tropical fruits and I just love making this salad dressing when it is in season and storing it in my refrigerator. Pour this over all your salads and enjoy a little bit of the tropics in every bite.

Makes: 1 cup (240 ml)
Cook Time: 5 minutes

½ cup (120 ml) avocado oil
1 shallot, diced
2 cloves (8 g) garlic, grated
½ tsp kosher salt
1 cup (240 ml) passionfruit pulp
2 tbsp (30 ml) coconut aminos
¼ cup (4 g) chopped cilantro
3 tbsp (45 ml) red wine vinegar

In a saucepan over medium heat, heat the avocado oil. Add the diced shallot. Cook until the shallot is soft, about 2 minutes, then add the garlic and kosher salt. Continue to cook for a few seconds, then remove from the heat and let cool completely.

Separate the passionfruit juice from the pulp by pressing the pulp into a wire-mesh strainer and collecting the juice in a jar. You may retain a few tablespoons (45 ml) of the pulp to add to the dressing if you like.

In a blender, add the shallot and garlic with all their cooking oil, the coconut aminos, chopped cilantro, passionfruit juice, red wine vinegar and a few tablespoons of the passionfruit pulp (if using). Blend until smooth, about 2 minutes. Alternatively, you may add all the ingredients to a Mason jar and shake to combine for a chunkier dressing.

Cover and store any remaining dressing in the refrigerator for up to 2 weeks.

NOTES: You may use fresh or frozen passionfruit pulp for this recipe.

If the dressing thickens after being stored in the refrigerator, simply let it sit at room temperature to "thaw," then shake to mix well.

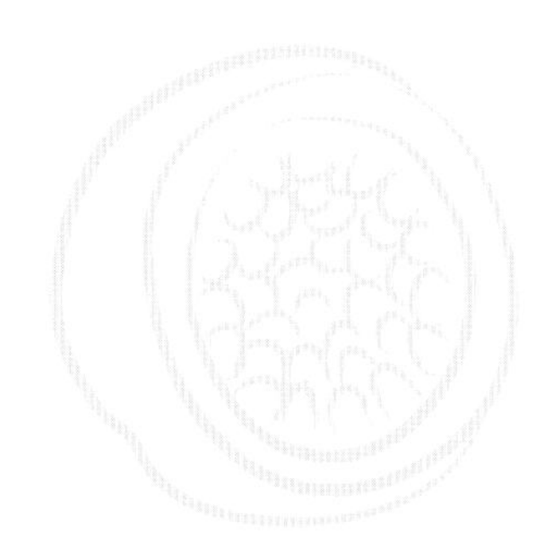

garam
masala

GARAM MASALA

Garam masala is a key ingredient in most Caribbean curries. You can find this spice blend in many mainstream supermarkets, but if you want to make your own at home, here is my recipe. However, it is sometimes more economical to buy a small bottle of garam masala than to source all the spices to make your own blend, especially if you're only using it for a few recipes.

Makes: 1 cup (100 g)
Cook Time: 10 minutes

½ cup (45 g) cumin seeds
¼ cup (20 g) coriander seeds
¼ cup (28 g) black peppercorns
4 cinnamon sticks
1 tbsp (5 g) cardamom seeds, cracked
1 tbsp (5 g) whole cloves
3 strands mace

In a skillet over medium-low heat, add the cumin seeds, coriander seeds, black peppercorns, cinnamon sticks, cardamom seeds, cloves and mace. Roast, stirring often, until the cumin seeds are dark in color, about 10 minutes. Keep the heat low to allow for even roasting. Allow the spices to cool completely, then transfer to a spice blender and blend until everything breaks down into a powder. Store the Garam Masala at room temperature in an airtight container, such as a Mason jar, for up to a month. After a month, it will still be good, but less potent.

CURRY POWDER

Curry powder is a spice blend used in Caribbean cooking. I grew up using Indi Madras curry powder in all my curries. Whenever my mom visits, she brings me a few packets that are hidden away in my pantry for my favorite curry dishes. When I am in a pinch and can't find Indi curry, I use whatever store-bought curry powder I can find, then I add some additional spices like ground coriander, turmeric, garam masala and geera to amp up the flavor. Sometimes I make my own curry powder blend at home, and you can too, using this recipe.

Makes: 1 cup (100 g)
Cook time: 10 minutes

2 tbsp (10 g) coriander seeds
2 tbsp (15 g) cumin seeds
1 tbsp (15 g) fenugreek seeds
¼ cup (27 g) ground turmeric
1 tbsp (8 g) garlic powder
1 tsp chili powder
½ tsp paprika
6 dried curry leaves (optional)

In a skillet over medium heat, add the coriander, cumin and fenugreek seeds. Toast until dark brown, stirring often for even cooking. Allow to cool completely, then place in a spice blender and blend until the spices become powder. To the powder, add ground turmeric, garlic powder, chili powder and paprika. Blend for 1 minute to combine. Pour in an airtight container and add the dried curry leaves (if using). Cover and store at room temperature for up to a month. I like to make my spice blends in small batches so that I can use them up quickly and they do not lose their potency.

WIRI WIRI RANCH DRESSING

This dressing and dipping sauce is a fusion of my love for spicy things and ranch. When I first made this ranch, I wanted to dip everything in it. It has all the goodness of traditional ranch but is dairy-free and spicy. It's great for times when you need some added fat and heat for your meals.

Makes: 1 cup (240 ml)
Cook Time: 5 minutes

½ cup (120 ml) coconut cream
1 cup (240 ml) Paleo-friendly mayonnaise
1 tbsp (15 ml) lime juice (about 1 lime)
1 tsp kosher salt
4 scallions
2 cloves (8 g) garlic
1 tbsp (3 g) parsley flakes
½ tsp smoked paprika
1–2 wiri wiri peppers or similar peppers like habanero or Scotch bonnet peppers

Into a blender cup or Mason jar large enough to fit your immersion blender and deep enough so that nothing spills over, add the coconut cream, mayonnaise, lime juice, kosher salt, scallions, garlic, parsley flakes, paprika and wiri wiri peppers. Blend until smooth or use your immersion blender in a steady up-and-down motion to slowly blend into a creamy and delicious spicy ranch. This takes 2 minutes or less.

Store in an airtight container in the refrigerator for 2 weeks. It may thicken over time, and if it does, simply rest at room temperature for 5 minutes and shake well before using.

MY CARIBBEAN PANTRY

Here are a few Caribbean pantry staples that may be unfamiliar to you. Some of you may already use these in your cooking, but it is still worth sharing how I use them. For example, coconut milk is a popular ingredient in Caribbean and Paleo cooking. When using canned coconut milk, I dilute it first for best results. I always have these staples on hand and use them in many of the recipes in this book. Most can be sourced at your chain supermarket. Others can be found at Mexican or Asian markets and the rest you can find on Amazon.

Coconut Aminos

I am so grateful for the magic that is coconut aminos. Made from coconut tree sap that is aged and fermented, coconut aminos are typically used as a soy sauce substitute, but this dark and slightly sweet sauce is a perfect addition to Caribbean cooking. A lot of Caribbean recipes start by adding sugar to a hot pan to make a caramel commonly called browning or burnt sugar. Coconut aminos are a perfect substitution. I use them in many of my recipes when I need a little bit of color and some sweetness to balance out acidity. You can find coconut aminos next to soy sauce and other Asian seasonings at your local supermarket or health food stores.

Coconut Milk

Coconut milk is an essential Caribbean ingredient. When I was growing up, we made fresh coconut milk by shelling dried coconuts, grating them and adding water. Rubbing the grated coconut between your palms was the easiest way to extract as much of the creamy coconut milk as possible, and this was my job. I prefer fresh coconut milk to canned. When using canned coconut milk, please dilute the milk using a 1:1 ratio with water—all the recipes in this book that use coconut milk have the equivalent amount of water in the ingredients list. One can of coconut milk to one can of water gives the best consistency for the recipes in this book.

Culantro

Culantro, also called chadon beni and bhandania, is an herb with a similar flavor profile to cilantro, but is more potent. It is popular in Trinidadian cooking, but also well-known throughout the Caribbean. You can find it at Asian markets. However, if you can't find it, feel free to use cilantro as a substitute.

Geera

Geera is roasted cumin. It is often called geera when it is ground but can also be called geera when it is whole. It is an essential spice in Caribbean curries. This single-ingredient ground spice is pretty simple to make. Cumin is roasted until dark and rich, then pounded in a mortar until smooth. My mom places hers between parchment paper and rolls it with her rolling pin. I can still remember the smell of spices being toasted as she made her weekly batch of geera. Of course, you can also add it to a spice blender!

Geera is very simple to make. Add 1 cup (96 g) of cumin seeds to a skillet over medium heat. Toss with a wooden spoon, spatula or simply by gently moving the skillet over the heat. Toast until dark in color and almost black. The darker the color, the richer the flavor, but be careful not to completely burn the cumin.

Remove from the heat and allow to cool before grinding. Place toasted cumin between two sheets of parchment paper and roll with a rolling pin until ground into a fine powder. Any cumin seeds that were missed in the toasting step will be hard to grind. Pour your geera in an airtight container like a Mason jar, cover and store at room temperature.

The shelf-life on this is very long, but be aware that toasted ground spices lose their flavor over time. Feel free to make it in smaller batches if needed.

Root and Other Veggies

I get excited when I stroll through the supermarket and I see familiar Caribbean vegetables and root vegetables (ground provisions, as we call them). I immediately think about all the things I can make. It is no surprise that root and other veggies play a key role in so many of the recipes in this book.

Cassava

Cassava is my second favorite ground provision. This starchy and creamy root vegetable will rival potatoes any day. It is often difficult to find cassava root in mainstream supermarkets and when you do find them they are almost always rotten. If after peeling your cassava root you notice bluish-gray veins or any soft or light pink part, that cassava is no longer good. Your best bet for getting good, raw cassava is to buy it frozen. I buy cassava from the freezer section of Mexican or Latinx markets and Asian markets.

If you manage to find good, fresh cassava, peeling it can be a bit tricky and you will lose most of the flesh if you use a vegetable peeler. To peel the cassava, start by cutting your cassava into manageable rounds. I typically do 3- to 4-inch (7.5- to 10-cm) rounds. Using a paring knife, make a vertical slit in the skin of the cassava. Next slide the tip of the knife in between the slit and under the skin. Peel away the skin until you can see the white flesh beneath. Repeat until all the pieces are peeled. You can then cut your cassava pieces down the middle for easy cooking.

Callaloo and Bhajie

In Guyana, callaloo and bhajie are used interchangeably to mean any leafy vegetable (except lettuce). Any variety of spinach is called callaloo. In Jamaica, callaloo refers only to green amaranth or Chinese spinach. In Trinidad and Tobago, callaloo specifically refers to a dish made with dasheen greens and okra. In this book, the Sautéed Callaloo recipe (page 90) refers to Jamaican callaloo or green amaranth. I get callaloo from my local Asian market. You may find the variety that has purple leaves. Both the purple and green varieties work well with the recipe. If you cannot find callaloo, feel free to use spinach as a substitute.

Eddoes (Dasheen)

In Guyana, we call a root vegetable that looks like small taro root an "eddoe." In most of the Caribbean, they call it dasheen. Eddoes are also sometimes called Malanga. While the Malanga I've bought in supermarkets aren't quite the eddoes we have at home in Guyana, they are a close substitute. In recipes where I use eddoes, feel free to substitute with taro or Malanga and in a worst-case scenario, potatoes.

Farine

Farine is short for the Brazilian farinha de mandioca. It is made by grating cassava root, extracting all the juices and then toasting it. The result is a grain-free ingredient with a grain-like texture. Farine is an indigenous ingredient, but it is so versatile and can take Paleo cooking to new heights. Farine is also known to Africans as gari or garri. If you live in a diverse community and have access to African markets, you can find farine there by asking for gari, or you can buy farine from Amazon. It comes in two varieties, white and yellow. Yellow farine has palm oil added to it. If this is an ingredient you avoid in your diet, please choose white farine. Both work exactly the same in the recipes in this book.

Marrid Man Poke

Marrid Man Poke is a type of basil found in Guyana. It is much stronger in smell and flavor than Italian basil. Unlike Italian basil, it does not lose its potency when cooked. It is used in many rice dishes and in green seasoning. It is closest in flavor to Thai basil; therefore, Thai basil is the best substitute for this herb.

Plantains

Before we go any further, Caribbean people say plantain like mountain, fountain and captain. Although plantains are technically not a root vegetable and are in the banana family (some people call them cooking bananas), they are often lumped in with ground provisions. I love plantains in any ripeness and form, from green, to green with a bit of yellow, to turning and then the varying stages of ripe. I can probably tell you 100 ways to prepare plantains and all of them will be delicious. When I was growing up, my dad bought a bunch of plantains every week and we cooked and ate to our hearts' content. Plantain is life! This is a true statement. They are so versatile and you can do many things with them.

In recipes, pay attention to the type of plantains you need. If you need ripe plantains, pay attention to the degree of ripeness as this will be crucial to the success of the dish. Is it yellow with no black spots? Is it black with just a few yellow spots? These are all very important distinctions.

Peeling ripe plantains is relatively easy, but peeling green plantains can be a bit tricky, so here is a quick how-to. Start by rubbing some oil on your hands, just enough to prevent that sticky residue from the plantain peel from staining your fingers. Then cut the tips off the plantain. With a paring knife, make lengthwise slits along the plantain. You can do this using the natural lines on the plantain skin as an easy guide. Next, slide the tip of the knife under the skin at the top of one of the slits and peel away that portion of skin. Repeat until you remove all the skin.

Peppers

Spicy hot peppers are a key part of Caribbean cooking, although if you don't like spice you can leave them out. You have my permission. In Guyana, wiri wiri peppers are a key part of our cuisine. They are small, berry-shaped peppers that pack a punch. Without the heat, they have a mild, fruity, aromatic flavor. I love removing the seeds and the veins for the flavor with just a hint of heat.

Wiri wiri peppers are not easily accessible. My mom sends me frozen wiri wiri peppers from New York and I keep them in the freezer, using them sparingly in recipes. When I don't have wiri wiri peppers, I use habanero peppers. The flavor is not identical, but the heat is just about the same (in my humble opinion).

If you have access to Scotch bonnet peppers (key peppers for Jamaicans) or pimento (key for Trinidadians), feel free to substitute these other peppers for wiri wiri peppers in my recipes. As a last resort, you can use cayenne pepper.

Pumpkin

In the Caribbean, we commonly call calabaza squash pumpkin. The variety that we grow and find in the Caribbean is green-skinned with some yellow spots. The variety that I find most often in the U.S. is pale orange-skinned (not like Halloween pumpkins). However, Guyanese people will cook anything that closely resembles pumpkin and call it squash. For recipes that include pumpkin, feel free to use butternut squash, kabocha squash, or if you're desperate, American pumpkin.

Sweet Potatoes

Caribbean sweet potatoes are not the same as American sweet potatoes. They are white fleshed with a pinkish-purple skin. They are the same as Japanese sweet potatoes. If you have access to an Asian market and can get Japanese sweet potatoes, this will be the closest to the sweet potatoes I am using in my recipes. If you can't find those, golden or white sweet potatoes are the next best bet.

ACKNOWLEDMENTS

It takes a village to write a book. I didn't know this when I started. I thought I could write and photograph this book over a few short months and carry on with business as usual with the raising of my three children and the running of the blog. I could not. My village stepped in and saved me. Together we created this book. There would be no book without them.

To my husband Sean, you are incredible and I am grateful that I get to share this journey with you. Thank you for always lifting me up, even when I had doubts that I could do it. Thank you for every time you cleaned the kitchen after I used every single utensil and pot during recipe testing and was too exhausted to lift a finger after. Thank you for loving all of me, even the messiest parts.

To my mother Sheena, you are the kindest, most giving human I know. Thank you for dropping everything and moving across the country when I needed you the most. Because of you, I was able to pour so much of me into this book, without feeling like I was failing at motherhood. You stepped in to take care of my family and my home when there weren't enough hours in the day to write and photograph a book and play chauffeur to three busy kids.

To my children who tried so many recipes and gave their unfiltered feedback, I am grateful for your candor and even more grateful for your willingness to try new foods.

To Kirth Bobb, words cannot describe how grateful I am to call you family. Thank you for saying yes without hesitation to photographing the cover and other portraits featured in this book. Thank you for your guidance and inspiration and for always telling me to "chill" when I was focusing on the things that weigh me down.

To my village of friends and family who showed up for me when I needed them, cheered me on along the way and created space for me when I needed it: THANK YOU!

To my blog community and metemgee family, thank you all for your continued support and for continually asking me for a cookbook. This book truly is for you.

Thank you to the team at Page Street Publishing for all the work you put in to making this book possible, especially to my editor and the design team. I am grateful that I have such an amazing team to guide me along the way.

ABOUT THE AUTHOR

Althea Brown is the creator and voice behind metemgee.com, a blog about Guyanese (Caribbean) recipes and traditions. She is also a Whole30 Certified Coach and was named Whole30's Coach Innovator of the Year in 2022. You can often find her on social media sharing stories about her food and culture, and as a frequent recipe contributor on Whole30's social media platforms.

After struggling with acid reflux for years, Althea started exploring the possibility that the way she ate was making her sick. Althea noticed that gluten was the main cause of her acid reflux and that gluten, dairy and refined sugar triggered the frequent migraines she had suffered from since adolescence. She started recreating her favorite Guyanese and Caribbean recipes to be gluten-, dairy- and refined sugar–free. Later she took the leap and started eliminating grains from her diet and noticed significant changes in her overall health. She hopes that she will continue to inspire everyone to try Caribbean food, even if it's through a slightly different lens.

Born and raised in Georgetown, Guyana, Althea now lives in Aurora, Colorado, with her husband and three children.

INDEX

D

E

F

G

H

I

J

L

M

N

O

P

R

S